HOLLYWOOD PUZZLES

Publications International, Ltd.

Let's get social!
@Publications_International
@PublicationsInternational
@BrainGames.TM
www.pilbooks.com

INTRODUCTION

Do you find yourself gathering all the gossip you can about your favorite film stars and their blockbuster movies? Are you interested in putting your knowledge to the test? Then it's time to exercise your body's most important organ—your brain—with *Brain Games®️ Hollywood Puzzles*.

This book contains a wide range of challenging puzzles, from crosswords and word searches to anagrams and cryptograms. More than 135 puzzles are included. Puzzle themes include well-known films, actors, and directors—both classic and contemporary.

So get your film fix from *Brain Games®️ Hollywood Puzzles*—mental calisthenics have never been this much fun!

MARVEL-OUS MOVIES

ACROSS

1. "____: The Dark World": 2013 film starring Chris Hemsworth

5. 3 on the phone

8. "The Incredible ____": 2008 film starring Lou Ferrigno

12. "Divorce capital," once

13. A hot time, in France

14. "____ penny, two a penny…"

15. Boats like the one Noah built

16. "… a lender be"

17. Architectural overhang

18. 2019 superhero film starring Brie Larson

21. Abbr. on a dashboard

22. Belgian painter James with "Scandalized Masks"

23. Arrange in advance

26. "Howards ____" (Forster novel)

27. "Fuzzy Wuzzy ____ a bear"

29. "Just the facts, ____"

30. Abbr. after a former military leader's name

31. Big name in building block toys

32. "Psychic" entertainer Geller

33. "All in favor" word

34. Coast Guard Academy student

35. Eyelash flutter

37. Bitterly cold

38. 2016 film starring Benedict Cumberbatch

43. Sean and Yoko

44. "____ a Most Unusual Day"

45. Epic poet

46. Baseball stitching

47. Brazil's ____ Paulo

48. "Idylls of the King" woman

49. Toward sunrise, in Mexico

50. "As needed," in Rx's

51. "And here you have it!"

DOWN

1. Gillette's ____ II razor

2. "Iliad" woman

3. Being punished, in a mess hall

4. Platform for public speaking

5. Blue jeans material

6. "Playing fields" place

7. State of unrest

8. Farmers tilling soil

9. Like promises never made

10. Power to influence people or things

11. "Kiss Kiss Bang Bang" critic Pauline

19. Angry Birds, for one

20. "____ the Band Played On" (1993 movie)

23. Campus in Dallas, TX

24. Hammer, anvil, and stirrup

25. Formal wear for Jeeves

26. AAA's opposite, in shoes

28. Falstaff, e.g.

30. Fiber-rich cracker brand

31. Wager

33. "It's ____-brainer!"

34. "Down on the Corner" band, affectionately

36. "Don't you recognize the voice?"

37. "I'm ready to rumble!"

38. Amount of medication

39. Red giant or white dwarf

40. "Peter Pan" pooch

41. You're filling one in

42. Norse epic

Answers on page 170.

RHYME TIME

Each clue leads to a 2-word answer that rhymes, such as BIG PIG or STABLE TABLE. The numbers in parentheses after the clue give the number of letters in each word. For example, "cookware taken from the oven (3, 3)" would be "hot pot."

1. Angry child at the movies (3, 3): _____

2. Celebrity at a distance (3, 4): _____

3. Clique within the cast (6, 5): _____

4. In search of comic relief (5, 8): _____

5. Part of a "Star Trek" episode (5, 5): _____

6. Previous year's performers (4, 4): _____

7. TV series finale (4, 9): _____

8. Aykroyd admirer (3, 3): _____

Answers on page 170.

ONE TIME

Find the word "film" once—and only once—in the grid below.

```
I L L M F I F M
L M L M M I M M
L L F F I I L M
L L M I M I L F
F L I I F L L F
I F L I L I M L
M I M M I F L M
M I F L F L I I
```

Answer on page 170.

THE DARK SIDE

Solve the clues below, and then place the letters in their corresponding spots in the grid to reveal a quote by Tim Burton. The letter in the upper-right corner of each grid square refers to the clue the letter comes from. A black square indicates the end of a word.

A. More than usual, like many Burton films

$\overline{\quad}$ $\overline{\quad}$ $\overline{\quad}$ $\overline{\quad}$ $\overline{\quad}$ $\overline{\quad}$
31   18   68   72   8   14

B. 2005 film "_____ Bride"

$\overline{\quad}$ $\overline{\quad}$ $\overline{\quad}$ $\overline{\quad}$ $\overline{\quad}$ $\overline{\quad}$
23   30   47   42   9   44

C. Exotic fruit

$\overline{\quad}$ $\overline{\quad}$ $\overline{\quad}$ $\overline{\quad}$ $\overline{\quad}$
19   82   66   20   64

D. 2001 Tim Burton remake of a classic: 4 wds.

$\overline{\quad}$ $\overline{\quad}$ $\overline{\quad}$ $\overline{\quad}$ $\overline{\quad}$ $\overline{\quad}$ $\overline{\quad}$ $\overline{\quad}$ $\overline{\quad}$ $\overline{\quad}$ $\overline{\quad}$
40   71   74   37   24   58   12   53   83   2   57

$\overline{\quad}$ $\overline{\quad}$ $\overline{\quad}$ $\overline{\quad}$
79   43   60   22

E. Spoiled, perhaps

$\overline{\quad}$ $\overline{\quad}$ $\overline{\quad}$ $\overline{\quad}$ $\overline{\quad}$ $\overline{\quad}$
29   4   28   85   45   78

F. 1988 Tim Burton hit "Beetle_____"

$\overline{\quad}$ $\overline{\quad}$ $\overline{\quad}$ $\overline{\quad}$ $\overline{\quad}$
7   73   84   69   50

G. Unparalleled technical skill

‾ ‾ ‾ ‾ ‾ ‾ ‾ ‾ ‾ ‾
35 17 54 15 41 34 6 21 32 52

H. 2003 tall-tale Burton flick: 2 wds.

‾ ‾ ‾ ‾ ‾ ‾ ‾
80 36 38 46 76 63 16

I. Recommended screening procedure

‾ ‾ ‾ ‾ ‾ ‾ ‾ ‾ ‾
65 26 49 13 81 67 61 39 56

J. Show place

‾ ‾ ‾ ‾ ‾ ‾ ‾
77 59 62 70 10 5 25

K. Spaghetti partner, sometimes

‾ ‾ ‾ ‾ ‾ ‾ ‾ ‾ ‾
33 3 48 1 51 55 75 27 11

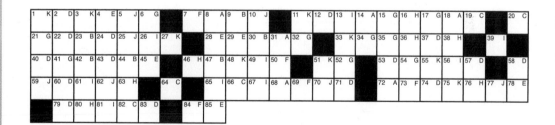

1 K	2 D	3 K	4 E	5 J	6 G		7 F	8 A	9 B	10 J		11 K	12 D	13 I	14 A	15 G	16 H	17 G	18 A	19 C		20 C
21 G	22 D	23 B	24 D	25 J	26 I	27 K		28 E	29 E	30 B	31 A	32 G		33 K	34 G	35 G	36 H	37 D	38 H		39 I	
40 D	41 G	42 B	43 D	44 B	45 E		46 H	47 B	48 K	49 I	50 F		51 K	52 G		53 D	54 G	55 K	56 I	57 D		58 D
59 J	60 D	61 I	62 J	63 H		64 C		65 I	66 C	67 I	68 A	69 F	70 J	71 D		72 A	73 F	74 D	75 K	76 H	77 J	78 E
	79 D	80 H	81 I	82 C	83 D		84 F	85 E														

Answers on page 170.

KNIVES OUT

ACROSS

1. Pretty-picture link

4. Many a soccer rooter

7. Emphatic ending with yes or no

12. Character of a fabric

14. Pretzels, basically

15. Sparks

16. Lofty objective

17. He was Benoit Blanc in "Knives Out"

19. Classic Buick

20. Banana castoff

23. Nobel-winning author Wiesel

24. Canon camera model

27. Riverbank word in "American Pie" lyrics

29. God, in the Quran

31. Cheer for the matador

32. Sunscreen compound

36. Full of uncertainties

37. Small taxi

39. Oscar category that Ana de Armas was nominated for

43. Salon overhaul

45. Sun parlors

46. Kilt pattern

47. Blackboard chore

48. Rolls's partner

49. License to drill, for short?

50. ____ out: scrape by

DOWN

1. Not much at all

2. Will be, in a 1956 hit song

3. Nerve impulse carrier

4. What the Louvre is, to a Parisian

5. Ultimatum words

6. Agave drink

7. Winter sports mecca

8. Sundance entry

9. "Walkabout" director Nicolas

10. JFK posting

11. Subj. for some bilinguals

13. Armor plate for the thigh

18. Cleanup hitter's goal, briefly

20. Old Mideast org.

21. Long-bodied swimmer

22. "Killing ____" (Sandra Oh spy drama)

24. Gnome cousin

25. Lumbering sort

26. Not forthcoming

28. Series unit

30. Many October babies

33. Morsel for a toad

34. Unfit to judge

35. Diplomatic agreement

37. Battlefield doc

38. Titan who holds up the heavens

39. NYC theater district

40. Lake by Ontario

41. Kitchen fixture

42. Wizard

43. "Tell Me More" network

44. "Mr. Blue Sky" band

Answers on page 170.

ELEVATOR WORDS

Like an elevator, words move up and down the "floors" of this puzzle. Starting with the first answer, the second part of each answer carries down to become the first part of the following answer. With the clues given, complete the puzzle.

1. Amazing _____

2. _____ _____

3. _____ _____

4. _____ _____

5. _____

6. _____

7. _____ control

1. Oft sung hymn

2. Classic Hollywood star and Princess of Monaco

3. Color worn on St. Paddy's Day

4. Background in front of which some actors perform

5. Movie script

6. Recreation area in the school-yard

7. It monitors and directs space-craft

12

Answers on page 171.

ADD-A-WORD

Add one word to each of the 3-word sets to create new words or phrases. For example: In a set including "smith," "fore," and "game," the added word would be "word" (creating "wordsmith," "foreword," and "word game").

1. set, noir, making: _____

2. aerial, list, head: _____

3. title, plot, text: _____

4. film, cut, neck: _____

5. actor, study, arc: _____

SAY WHAT?

Below is a group of words that, when properly arranged in the blanks, reveal a quote from Orson Welles.

down worked started way top

I _____ at the _____ and _____ my

_____ _____.

13

Answers on page 171.

LEADING MEN

This word search has an extra twist. Use the list of clues to figure out each actor hidden in the grid. Names can be found in a straight line horizontally, vertically, or diagonally. They may read either forward or backward.

1. Joaquin ___ won Best Actor Oscar for *Joker*.

2. Starred in *Ford v Ferrari* and *The Dark Knight*.

3. Nominated for Oscars in *La La Land* and *Half Nelson*.

4. Played Freddie Mercury in *Bohemian Rhapsody*.

5. Won Best Supporting Actor Oscar for *Once Upon a Time… In Hollywood*.

6. Starred in *At Eternity's Gate*, *The Lighthouse*, and *The Florida Project*.

7. Won Best Actor Oscars for *Forrest Gump* and *Philadelphia*.

8. Leonardo ___ starred in *The Wolf of Wall Street* and *Titanic*.

9. Won Oscars for *Moonlight* and *Green Book*.

10. Starred in *Marriage Story* and *BlacKkKlansman*.

11. Co-wrote and starred in *Good Will Hunting*.

12. Played Tom Hayden in *The Trial of the Chicago 7*.

```
E E Y T O M H A N K S L C
N O R B N A I T S I R H C
Y T E P A H S F D W R O H
A T V H H E X W O I Y I V
M I I O M R M P S L A R N
D P R E O S K T W L N P O
E D D N T H I I I E G A M
R A M I M A L E K M O C A
E R A X N L Y B X D S I D
I B D B E A C V B A L D T
D G A M E A C X V F I P T
D L D V E L B P H O N L A
E A L A M I M A R E G C M
```

Answers on page 171.

GREAT LINES FROM THE MOVIES

Cryptograms are messages in substitution code. Break the code to read the famous movie quotes and the movies that featured them. For example, THE SMART CAT might be FVO QWGDF JGF if F is substituted for T, V for H, O for E, and so on. Hint: Look for repeated letters. E, T, A, O, N, R, and I are the most often used letters. A single letter is usually A or I; OF, IS, and IT are common 2-letter words; THE and AND are common 3-letter words. The code is the same for all four quotes.

1. "DVLNAVQ, RS DJOS J HIVUTSE." —JHVTTV 13

2. "B NSS WSJW HSVHTS." —ADS NBGAD NSQNS

3. "NDVR ES ADS EVQSK!" —MSIIK EJZLBIS

4. "NJK DSTTV AV EK TBAATS PIBSQW." —NYJIPJYS

Answers on page 171.

B_NG J_ _N H_ F_LMS

Below is a list of some films Bong Joon Ho directed. The only thing is, they've lost A, E, I, O, and U, as well as any punctuation and spaces between words. Can you figure out the missing vowels and name each film in the list below?

1. T H H S T

2. M M R S F M R D R

3. M T H R

4. K J

5. P R S T

6. S N W P R C R

Answers on page 171.

EITHER/OR

What 2 words, formed from different arrangements of the same 8 letters, can be used to complete the sentence below?

She watched the movie "From Here to _____"

in its _____.

PASSING A BIRD'S HOME

Can you "read" the film title below?

1FLU

CUCKOO'S HOME

Answers on page 171.

CODE-DOKU

Solve this puzzle just like a sudoku. Use deductive logic to complete the grid so that each row, column, and 2 by 2 box contains the letters from the film title JAWS only once.

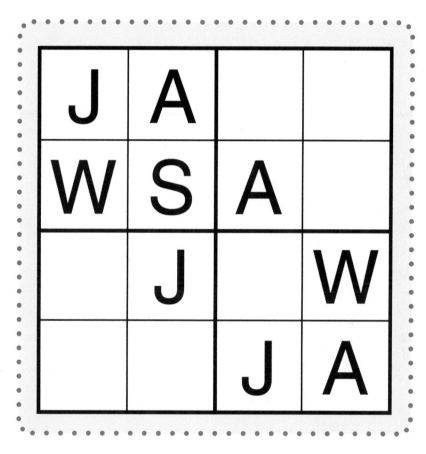

Answers on page 171.

ADAM DRIVER FILMS

ACROSS

1. "Pirates of the Caribbean" series star

5. "Aladdin" prince

8. A/C rating units

12. "Adios," in Italy

13. "Mad Men" actor Hamm

14. ____ buco (veal dish)

15. About, in contracts

16. "Just do it" or "Got milk?"

18. Adam Driver was FBI agent Daniel Jones in this 2019 political drama

20. Animation frames

21. "Isn't that cute?" sounds

22. Like a needle or a nut

25. "The Color of Money" prop

28. Driver played stage director Charlie Barber in this 2019 movie with Scarlett Johansson

31. Hoppin' mad feeling

32. Zinfandel, e.g.

33. Biblical floating zoo

35. A long, long time

36. Driver was Lev Shapiro in this 2012 film with Greta Gerwig

39. "Evidently!"

41. "Clown of the orchestra"

44. Modern encyclopedia platform

45. "Blueberries for ____" (classic children's book)

46. Arm bone

47. Arch molding

48. "Tinker, Tailor, Soldier, ____"

49. Be at ease

DOWN

1. 601, in old Rome

2. "A" in German class

3. Ornamental garden or theater section

4. Comic actress Amy

5. "When is a door not a door? When it's ____"

6. Bonanza vein

7. To a great degree

8. Churlish chaps

9. Air Force NCO

10. Chant at the Olympics

11. "Dombey and ____" (Dickens)

17. Gear for going up hills

19. Actor Morales of "Paid in Full"

20. Arctic trout

22. "Don't need those details!"

23. Conrad's "Heart of ____"

24. "It's all about me" trait

25. Like silver and gold

26. Banquet coffeepots

27. "Good ____!" (praise for a batter)

29. Keeps company with

30. Like some parking

33. Beloved PGA nickname

34. "King ____" (James Clavell novel)

36. Not bona fide

37. Be a good fan

38. Jed Clampett's daughter

39. "Letters From ____ Jima": 2006 film

40. Bummed smoke

42. Carry-____ (some luggage)

43. "All you can ____" (buffet sign)

WALK OF FAME

Change just one letter on each line to go from the top word to the bottom word. Do not change the order of the letters. You must have a common English word at each step.

WALK

_____ speak

_____ story

_____ subdue

FAME

LETTER TILES

Using the letter tiles, create 10 four-letter words. Create 20, and you're a Word Sleuth; create 30, and you're a Word Wonder; create 40, and you're a Word Master!

B L O C K B U S T E R

Answers on page 172.

2 THUMBS UP

Pop some popcorn, fill up a gallon jug with soda, and pretend you're at the movies as you fill in the blanks to complete the titles of these classic films:

1. The Hills Have . . .
   a. Peaks
   b. Billies
   c. Eyes
   d. Brothers

2. The Treasure of the Sierra . . .
   a. Mazda
   b. Madras
   c. Madre
   d. Mondays

3. From Here to . . .
   a. There
   b. Maternity
   c. Virginity
   d. Eternity

4. Close Encounters of the Third . . .
   a. Reich
   b. Kind
   c. Base
   d. Wave

5. A Streetcar Named...
   a. Perspire
   b. Flat Tire
   c. Retire
   d. Desire

6. His Girl . . .
   a. Dumped Him
   b. Pearl
   c. Friday
   d. Robot

7. Inherit the . . .
   a. Money
   b. Air
   c. Problems
   d. Wind

8. In the Heat of the...
   a. Hot Tub
   b. Beat
   c. Day
   d. Night

9. The African . . .
   a. Queen
   b. Prince
   c. Elephant
   d. American

10. The Thin . . .
   a. Ice
   b. Man
   c. Mint
   d. Dime

Answers on page 172.

BEST ACTRESS WINNERS

ACROSS

1. NFL quarterback Newton

4. ____ Stone, Best Actress for "La La Land," 2016

8. ____ Larson, Best Actress for "Room," 2015

12. "Bravo!" at a bullfight

13. Eager desire

14. "Game of Thrones" actress Headey

15. "ASAP!"

16. Beach shovel go-with

17. Mine finds

18. Best Actress for "Still Alice," 2014

21. "... the law is a ____" (Dickens quote)

22. Full ranges

23. Real-estate ad abbr.

26. "A lie that makes us realize truth," per Picasso

27. Acapulco uncle

28. Grande and Bravo

29. "Blueprint for a Sunrise" singer

30. 12-time Pro Bowl linebacker Junior

31. "Was ____ das?" (German "What is that?")

32. Browning's "____ Vogler"

33. Center spot

34. ____ l'oeil (literally, "deceive the eye")

36. Dress (up) fancily

37. Best Actress for "Blue Jasmine," 2013

42. Beneficiary of a will

43. "Everything's fine!"

44. Far from forward

45. Beverly Hillbilly ____ May Clampett

46. In ____ (as first placed)

47. Bobby of ice hockey

48. Cat's sunning spot

49. "____ Calm and Carry On"

50. "Born," in wedding notices

DOWN

1. "And" or "or": abbr.

2. Baseball brother Felipe or Matty

3. Cry like a kitten

4. Northeast toll road convenience

5. No visible ____ of support

6. Disney World's ____ Street U.S.A.

7. Brisk, in music

8. Actress Claire

9. Shunted elsewhere

10. They keep you going

11. Departs unobtrusively

19. Alpo rival

20. "Welcome" rug

23. Too big for one's ____

24. British Prime Minister Benjamin

25. Turn soil by machine

26. Underground colonist

29. Cleopatra's Needle, for one

30. "Oh, well" noise

32. "Be on the lookout" letters

33. Model used for study or testing

35. ____ Streep, Best Actress for "The Iron Lady," 2011

36. Certain govt. security

38. Bordeaux girlfriend

39. "The dismal science," for short

40. Burned rubber

41. Ancient city whose name means "rock"

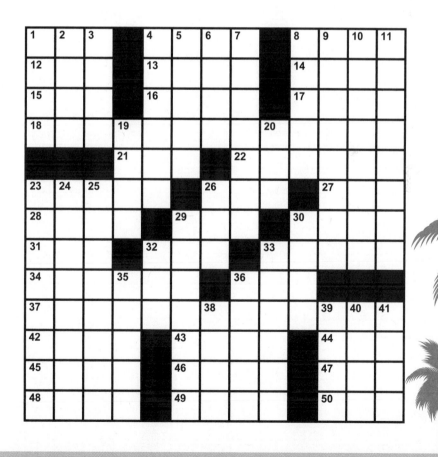

Answers on page 172.

A TUNEFUL LOVE STORY

Solve the clues below, and then place the letters in their corresponding spots in the grid to reveal a quote from the film "Meet Me in St. Louis." The letter in the upper-right corner of each grid square refers to the clue the letter comes from. A black square indicates the end of a word.

A. "Clang, clang, clang went _____"

<u> </u> <u> </u> <u> </u> <u> </u> <u> </u> <u> </u> <u> </u> <u> </u> <u> </u> <u> </u>
38 72 9 71 48 76 29 67 15 11

B. Panda food

<u> </u> <u> </u> <u> </u> <u> </u> <u> </u> <u> </u>
75 5 51 19 47 18

C. "Have _____ a Merry Little Christmas"

<u> </u> <u> </u> <u> </u> <u> </u> <u> </u> <u> </u> <u> </u> <u> </u>
22 53 13 6 64 45 30 69

D. Enlarging in appearance

<u> </u> <u> </u> <u> </u> <u> </u> <u> </u> <u> </u> <u> </u> <u> </u> <u> </u> <u> </u>
1 43 14 57 50 31 26 61 33 24

E. Judy's role

<u> </u> <u> </u> <u> </u> <u> </u> <u> </u> <u> </u>
70 78 59 8 42 54

F. Cried "Yee-haw!"

<u> </u> <u> </u> <u> </u> <u> </u> <u> </u> <u> </u> <u> </u>
7 60 12 27 52 49 34

G. Esther's beau: John _____

—	—	—	—	—	—
55	44	36	40	58	17

H. Showing hospitality to

—	—	—	—	—	—	—	—	—	—
4	62	37	25	41	16	23	65	74	32	10

—
63

I. Duet sung by Mr. and Mrs. Smith: 3 wds.

—	—	—	—	—	—	—
77	35	28	73	66	3	68

J. Utter chaos

—	—	—	—	—	—
21	56	2	39	20	46

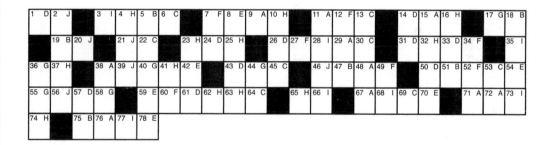

Answers on page 172.

CRYPTO-QUOTES

Cryptograms are messages in substitution code. Break the code to read the famous quotes from *The Wizard of Oz*. For example, THE SMART CAT might be FVO QWGDF JGF if F is substituted for T, V for H, O for E, and so on. Hint: Look for repeated letters. E, T, A, O, N, R, and I are the most often used letters. A single letter is usually A or I; OF, IS, and IT are common 2-letter words; THE and AND are common 3-letter words. The code is the same for all three quotes.

1. "PCPC, D'ES N XSSADGZ QS'HS

   GCP DG YNGWNW NGROCHS."

2. "D'AA ZSP RCT, OR IHSPPR,

   NGK RCTH ADPPAS KCZ, PCC!"

3. "PMSHS'W GC IANLS ADYS

   MCOS."

Answers on page 172.

ANAGRAMS

Unscramble each anagram (rearrangement) below to reveal a film starring Elizabeth Taylor.

1. PALACE ROT

2. INVOLVE A TALENT

3. ALIENATES PUNCH

4. FRESHMEN WITH A GHETTO

5. IF DISFAVORING A WHARF, WOO OIL

6. SLANDERED MUSTY SLUM

7. ATTRACTION ON HOOF

8. TEARY CENTURION

9. SHARPENED TIP

10. TAG IN

Answers on page 173.

THE BREAKFAST CLUB

ACROSS

1. He played "the athlete" Andy in "The Breakfast Club"

8. Gridlock cause

9. Place to wash up

10. Brazilian vacation spot

11. Optional courses

13. Ally, who played "the basket case" Allison in "The Breakfast Club"

15. Judd, who played "the criminal" John in "The Breakfast Club"

18. Source of sweets

19. "Dig in!"

20. Like luxury car interiors

22. Gliding ballroom dance

23. She played "the princess" Claire in "The Breakfast Club"

DOWN

1. Gets by coercion

2. Baking potato

3. Short stop or second baseman

4. Go over

5. Key for indenting

6. In relation to

7. Cheap shots, e.g.

12. "Those Were the Days," to "All in the Family"

14. Chinese appetizer

16. Journalist's tablet

17. Drink with an umbrella, often

18. Play a ukelele

19. Actor in a crowd

21. "That's great news!"

Answers on page 173.

SUCCESS BECOMES HER

Every word listed is contained within the group of letters. Words can be found in a straight line horizontally, vertically, or diagonally. They may read either forward or backward. Leftover letters reveal what Meryl Streep did shortly after winning an Oscar for *Kramer vs. Kramer*.

ACCENTS	JULIA
ADAPTATION	KRAMER VS. KRAMER
DEATH BECOMES HER	MAMMA MIA!
DEER HUNTER (The)	MANHATTAN
DEVIL WEARS PRADA (The)	OSCARS
DINGO	PRIME
DOUBT	RIVER WILD (The)
EVENING	SEAGULL (The)
HEARTBURN	SILKWOOD
HOURS (The)	SOPHIE'S CHOICE
IRONWEED	YALE

Leftover Letters: _____

```
K A C C D I L L U G A E S
R R I V E R W I L D D D E
A N T A A I M A M M A M L
M N A T T A H N A M R L Y
E C I O H C S E I H P O S
R T L E B D I N G O S G N
V F B H E A R T B U R N O
S T H U C E I R O R A I I
K R D O O W K L I S E N T
R S A C M D A R U O W E A
A A C C E N T S N J L V T
M T H M S E B A C A I E P
E K I O H O F A Y T V O A
R R I R E T N U H R E E D
P L E I R O N W E E D T A
```

 Answers on page 173.

HOLLYWOOD NICE GUY

Solve the clues below, and then place the letters in their corresponding spots in the grid to reveal a quote from Tom Hanks. The letter in the upper-right corner of each grid square refers to the clue the letter comes from. A black square indicates the end of a word.

A. Realistic

$\overline{}$ $\overline{}$ $\overline{}$ $\overline{}$ $\overline{}$
84   60   38   18   79

B. 1998 film "_____ Mail"

$\overline{}$ $\overline{}$ $\overline{}$ $\overline{}$ $\overline{}$ $\overline{}$ $\overline{}$ $\overline{}$
26   27   24   31   41   22   50   55

C. Lie

$\overline{}$ $\overline{}$ $\overline{}$ $\overline{}$ $\overline{}$ $\overline{}$ $\overline{}$
47   72   74   83   28   66   29

D. Hanks's 1995 animated film

$\overline{}$ $\overline{}$ $\overline{}$ $\overline{}$ $\overline{}$ $\overline{}$ $\overline{}$ $\overline{}$
33   12   67   35   56   71   15   78

E. Heart part

$\overline{}$ $\overline{}$ $\overline{}$ $\overline{}$ $\overline{}$
19   65   2   4   57

F. Forrest Gump's college sport

$\overline{}$ $\overline{}$ $\overline{}$ $\overline{}$ $\overline{}$ $\overline{}$ $\overline{}$ $\overline{}$
46   34   14   9   23   42   48   77

G. Beat through cleverness

$\overline{61}$ $\overline{36}$ $\overline{63}$ $\overline{6}$ $\overline{20}$ $\overline{73}$

H. Imaginary friend in "Cast Away"

$\overline{45}$ $\overline{10}$ $\overline{17}$ $\overline{81}$ $\overline{52}$ $\overline{43}$

I. Private Gump's platoon leader: _____ Dan

$\overline{49}$ $\overline{1}$ $\overline{32}$ $\overline{76}$ $\overline{25}$ $\overline{5}$ $\overline{21}$ $\overline{8}$ $\overline{62}$ $\overline{51}$

J. Park or 5th

$\overline{16}$ $\overline{40}$ $\overline{82}$ $\overline{58}$ $\overline{69}$ $\overline{85}$

K. Theme in "Road to Perdition" and (to a lesser extent) "Forrest Gump"

$\overline{53}$ $\overline{44}$ $\overline{59}$ $\overline{7}$ $\overline{80}$ $\overline{37}$ $\overline{64}$ $\overline{68}$ $\overline{3}$ $\overline{11}$

L. Fearful

$\overline{54}$ $\overline{13}$ $\overline{75}$ $\overline{30}$ $\overline{39}$ $\overline{70}$

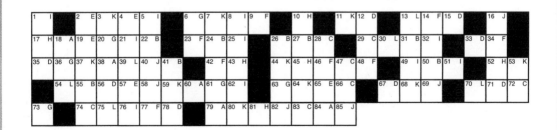

Answers on page 173.

ADD-A-WORD

Add one word to each of the 3-word sets to create new words or phrases. For example: In a set including "smith," "fore," and "game," the added word would be "word" (creating "wordsmith," "foreword," and "word game").

1. play, silver, test: _____

2. drop, flash, lot: _____

3. line, board, love: _____

4. cast, writer, arche: _____

5. film, up, piece: _____

6. back, green, box: _____

BEN-HUR

Change just one letter on each line to go from the top word to the bottom word. Do not change the order of the letters. You must have a common English word at each step.

BEN

_____

_____

HUR

Answers on pages 173 & 174.

SAY WHAT?

Below is a group of words that, when properly arranged in the blanks, reveal a quote from Elizabeth Taylor.

horses leading Some dogs my men

_____ of _____ best _____ _____ have been _____ and

_____.

ADDAGRAM

This puzzle functions exactly like an anagram with an added step: In addition to being scrambled, each word or phrase below is missing the same letter. Discover the missing letter, then unscramble the words. When you do, you'll reveal 4 movies from the 1990s.

DISORDERS HANDSAWS

SHRILL DISSENT

SELL USE

TITIAN

Answers on page 174.

DIRECTED BY CLINT EASTWOOD

ACROSS

1. Eastwood directed and stars as Preacher in 1985's "____ Rider," the highest-grossing Western of the decade

5. About-to-be-grads or AARP members, briefly

8. Bickering bout

12. Classic '80s sports car

13. "I'm amazed!"

14. 175-year-old canal

15. It goes up in a downpour

17. "A ____ formality!"

18. This 1992 Eastwood-directed Western won wide acclaim and four Academy Awards, including Best Picture

20. 1938 Sartre novel

23. Big ____ (David Ortiz nickname)

24. 911 respondent, briefly

25. Get the wrong signals from

28. Eastwood produced, directed, and acted (as a master jewel thief) in this 1997 political action thriller

32. Pastry chef's forms

33. Pitching number with a decimal

34. Alternative to "ja"

35. Having no pattern

38. Though named after a muscle car, this 2008 Clint Eastwood drama is not a racing movie

41. A great many

42. Dish-drying cloth

46. Melancholy woodwind

47. "The Lord of the Rings" tree being

48. This 1988 Eastwood-directed movie is a fond tribute to jazz saxophonist Charlie Parker

49. "Sesame Street" regular

50. Agcy. for narcs

51. British men of title

DOWN

1. More, in music scores

2. A slot machine has one

3. Arced, soft throw

4. Beige shades

5. Scale syllables

6. Candy in a tube

7. Permanent marker brand

8. Minor-league, maybe

9. Watched ahead of time

10. "Billion" suffix

11. "Happy Days" extra

16. Chicago-to-Toronto dir.

19. ("I'm shocked!")

20. A type of tide

21. Both (prefix)

22. Warren or Romney, e.g.

25. Geog. high points

26. "Flying" start

27. ⅛ fluid ounce

29. Mathematical collection that isn't closed

30. Au ____ (with milk)

31. Not seen

35. Calf roper's rope

36. Kitchen intruder

37. Neophytes, in slang

38. Amount of goop

39. After-bath garment

40. Thinker Descartes

43. Big name in video games

44. Exhibit one's humanity

45. Church of the Mormons: abbr.

Answers on page 174.

LEADING LADIES

This word search has an extra twist. Use the list of clues to figure out each actress hidden in the grid. Names can be found in a straight line horizontally, vertically, or diagonally. They may read either forward or backward.

1. Scarlett _____ starred in *Marriage Story* and *Jojo Rabbit*.

2. Won Oscars for *Sophie's Choice* and *The Iron Lady*.

3. Cynthia _____ played the title role in *Harriet*.

4. Won Best Actress Oscar for *La La Land*.

5. Starred in *Little Women* and *Lady Bird*.

6. Brie ___ won Best Actress Oscar for *Room*.

7. Starred opposite Bradley Cooper in *A Star Is Born*.

8. Olivia _____ won Best Actress for *The Favourite*.

9. Played the title role in *Erin Brockovich*.

10. Renée _____ won Best Actress for her portrayal of Judy Garland.

11. Starred in *Arrival* and *American Hustle*.

12. Played Virginia Woolf in *The Hours*.

13. Charlize _____ starred in *Monster* and *Bombshell*.

```
H N J S M A D A Y M A U C
Y S A O I R S E R O N A N
V T H M H N A E I B L L N
Z R J E D A A M Y C A A I
P E U R M I N M Y C R D C
P B L Y P M K S L U S Y O
O O I L J A A E S O D G L
T R A S W O L S L O C A E
H A R T E E H A T O N G K
E I O R C R G A R O C A I
R L B E E O I E N S N I D
O U E E U C L V R S O E N
N J V P J K P M O V S N K
```

SCRAMBLEGRAM

Four 7-letter words, all of which revolve around the same theme, have been jumbled. Unscramble each word, and write the answer in the accompanying space. Next, transfer the letters in the shaded boxes into the shaded keyword spaces, and unscramble the 6-letter word that goes with the theme. The theme for this puzzle is leading men, past and present.

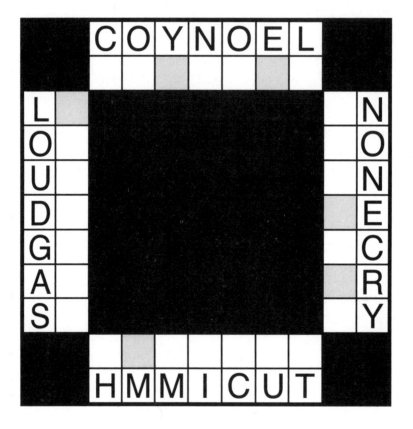

KEYWORD

Answers on page 174.

MORE GREAT LINES FROM THE MOVIES

Cryptograms are messages in substitution code. Break the code to read the famous movie quotes and the movies that featured them. For example, THE SMART CAT might be FVO QWGDF JGF if F is substituted for T, V for H, O for E, and so on. Hint: Look for repeated letters. E, T, A, O, N, R, and I are the most often used letters. The code is the same for all quotes.

1. "PB QJSQN, RQES RM NQM."
   —VONNST CRGQUD

2. "TBIBNM GODV IQIM CT DJS UBATSA." —NCADM NQTUCTP

3. "DJSAS'V TB UAMCTP CT IQVSIQYY!" —Q YSQPOS BW DJSCA BFT

4. "MBO UQT'D JQTNYS DJS DAODJ!" —Q WSF PBBN RST

ONCE UPON A TIME... IN HOLLYWOOD

ACROSS

1. Soft drink choice

5. Life force in Chinese philosophy

8. More than willing

12. Like some cheeses and wines

13. Solo of space opera

14. Bone up quickly

15. He plays Cliff Booth, Rick Dalton's stunt double, in "Once Upon a Time... in Hollywood"

17. Incur a bleep

18. Alum-to-be

19. Vote in

21. Crisp quality

22. Element of one's inheritance

23. Sing your own praises

26. Apple Records founders

29. "u r hilarious!"

30. Blue cartoon critter

32. Verb ending in old verse

33. Knocks over

35. Officially give up

36. Song from "Carmen," say

37. Fundraising sch. group

39. Boric and citric

40. Ill will

44. Like long chances

45. ____ DiCaprio plays actor Rick Dalton in the Tinseltown hit

47. Sicily's tallest mountain

48. Newcomer's study: abbr.

49. She kills Jabba the Hutt

50. Warm winter wear

51. Holy jurisdiction

52. E-mail screen button

DOWN

1. Some red wines, casually

2. Fairy-tale meanie

3. With less fat

4. Abacus activity

5. Cricket call

6. Beanie or beret

7. 98, but not 98.6

8. Southern drawl, e.g.

9. Martial arts legend played by Mike Moh in "Once Upon a Time... in Hollywood"

10. Bottom position

11. Ammonium has three

16. Island finger food

20. Foliage element

23. Diner sandwich inits.

24. Pouch-dwelling Pooh pal

25. He plays casting agent Marvin Schwarz in "Once Upon a Time . . . in Hollywood"

26. Airport shuttle

27. Airport gate posting, for short

28. Pronoun for any vessel

30. Hit a slick spot

31. Children's malady, often

34. Like some screams or urges

35. Gondola routes

37. Blue-collar worker

38. Loafer color

39. Member of the chorus

41. Canadian native

42. Viking god

43. It's between the shoulders

44. Put on a button, say

46. Tampa-to-Miami dir.

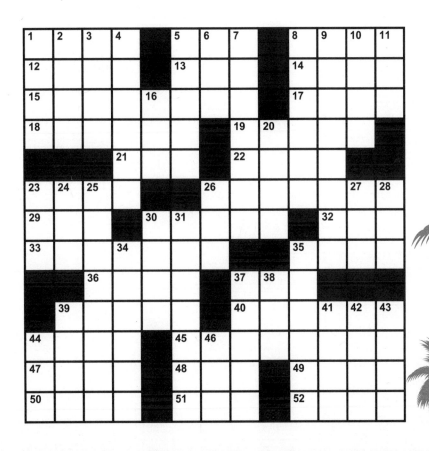

Answers on page 175.

ELEVATOR WORDS

Like an elevator, words move up and down the "floors" of this puzzle. Starting with the first answer, the second part of each answer carries down to become the first part of the following answer. With the clues given, complete the puzzle.

1. Inside _____

2. _____ _____

3. _____ _____

4. _____

5. _____ _____

6. _____ _____

7. _____ Heart

1. 2015 Pixar film

2. Dead to the world

3. 2003 Jude Law-Nicole Kidman film

4. Summit of the peak

5. 1986 Tom Cruise action flick

6. 1950 film noir about an armed robbery spree

7. 2009 movie starring Jeff Bridges

Answers on page 175.

WORD LADDER

Change just one letter on each line to go from the top word to the bottom word. Do not change the order of the letters. You must have a common English word at each step.

CAST

_____ container

_____ be concerned

_____ get along

_____ cultivate

_____ law practice

FILM

Answers on page 175.

MOVIES FROM A TO Z

Every movie title listed is contained within the group of letters. Titles can be found in a straight line horizontally, vertically, or diagonally. They may read either forward or backward.

AMISTAD	NON-STOP
BLACK PANTHER	OFFICE SPACE
CHANGELING	PULP FICTION
DIE HARD	QUIET PLACE (A)
ENIGMA	ROCKETMAN
FINDING DORY	SHREK
GHOST	TENET
HONEYBOY	UNCUT GEMS
ICARUS	VICE
JUST MERCY	WITNESS
KING KONG	X-MEN
LEGEND	YUMA
MILK	ZERO DARK THIRTY

```
L I M Y P U L P F I C T I O N
E Y T R I H T K R A D O R E Z
J N S O F F I C E S P A C E B
Q X I D S H R E W I T N E S S
U M M G Y L E N I G M A V D Q
I E A N C C H A N G E L I N G
E N Y I R T T M A H Y S C O S
T A U D E E N T G O O C A N M
P A M N M N A E N S B A R S E
L H I I T E P K O T Y M U T G
A E L F S T K C K H E U S O T
C I K X U T C O G V N Y O P U
E D I M J R A R N S O H G F C
C D N E G E L D I E H A R D N
F S H R E K B E K K E C I V U
```

Answers on page 175.

LOVE IS IN THE AIR

Cryptograms are messages in substitution code. Break the code to read a quote from Billy Crystal in "When Harry Met Sally." For example, THE SMART CAT might be FVO QWGDF JGF if F is substituted for T, V for H, O for E, and so on. Hint: Look for repeated letters. E, T, A, O, N, R, and I are the most often used letters.

"T WLXV OVKV QJZTYOQ

EVWLMBV GOVZ SJM KVLFTAV

SJM GLZQ QJ BCVZN QOV KVBQ

JI SJMK FTIV GTQO BJXVEJNS,

SJM GLZQ QOV KVBQ JI SJMK

FTIV QJ BQLKQ LB BJJZ LB

CJBBTEFV."

Answers on page 175.

CHICK FLICK

Move each of the letters below into the grid to form common words. You will use each letter once. The letters in the numbered cells of the grid correspond to the letters in the phrase at the bottom. Completing the grid will help you complete the phrase and vice versa. When finished, the grid and phrase should be filled with valid words, and you will have used all the letters in the letter set.

Hint: The numbered cells in the grid are arranged alphabetically, so the letter in the cell marked 1 will appear in the alphabet before the letter in the cell marked 2, and so on.

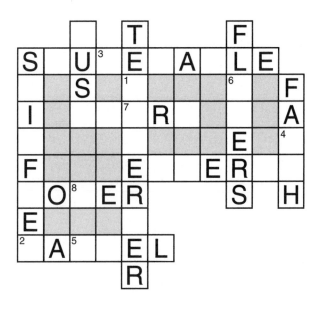

Answers on page 176.

BEST ACTOR WINNERS

ACROSS

1. ____ Malek, Best Actor for "Bohemian Rhapsody," 2018

5. "A Christmas Carol" exclamation

8. Thai coin

12. "Mr. Holland's ____" (1995 Dreyfuss film)

13. 4×4 vehicle, for short

14. A tiny amount

15. Like a multipurpose tool, perhaps

17. Margaret Mitchell classic, briefly

18. Best Actor for "Darkest Hour," 2017

20. "Every dog ____ its day"

21. Bartlett fruit

22. "7 Faces of Dr. ____" (1964 Tony Randall film)

25. Piece of clothing

28. Best Actor for "The Theory of Everything," 2014

32. Printer's type excess

33. Amazed admiration

34. "There's no I in ____"

35. Ballplayers who only bat, briefly

38. Best Actor for "The King's Speech," 2010

41. Bygone Bombay bigwig

42. Despite that

45. "Once ____ a Mattress" (old Broadway musical)

46. A shuttlecock sails over it

47. 1 and 66: abbr.

48. "Hopalong Cassidy" star William

49. Dundee's Firth of ____

50. Author Vonnegut

DOWN

1. "Balderdash!"

2. "Gorillas in the Mist" primate

3. Bean-sprout bean

4. Basketball Hall-of-Famer Thomas

5. Floats in the harbor

6. "... ____ extra charge!"

7. Comfy shoe insert

8. Judith Anderson's "Cat on a Hot Tin Roof" role

9. Informal greeting

10. "Now hear this!": abbr.

11. Child's fancy marble

16. 2nd Amendment grp.

19. Prefix meaning "skin"

22. "The Lip" Durocher

23. It modifies a v.

24. Highlight of Beethoven's Ninth Symphony

25. "____ Shorty": Elmore Leonard novel

26. Dir. opposite SSE

27. "Time out" signal shape

29. Country without snakes

30. "Chicago P.D." actor Morales

31. Carpet leftover

35. Little tune

36. Abbr. for a king or queen

37. Baby deliverer of legend

38. "The Godfather" boss

39. Biting bug

40. "Hotel Rwanda" tribe

41. "Ay, there's the ____" (Shakespeare)

43. Lang. that gives us "blitz"

44. "The buck stops here" presidential monogram

Answers on page 176.

MAY THE FORCE BE WITH YOU

Every word listed is contained within the group of letters. Words can be found in a straight line horizontally, vertically, or diagonally. They may read either forward or backward. Leftover letters spell the end of a quote from the know-it-all droid C-3PO that begins: "Don't worry about Master Luke. I'm sure he's all right…"

ANAKIN

CLONE

COUNT DOOKU

DARK SIDE

DARTH VADER

DEATH STAR

DROID

EMPIRE (The)

ENDOR

EWOKS

FORCE (The)

GALAXY

HAN SOLO

JABBA THE HUTT

JAR JAR BINKS

JEDI

LANDO

LEIA

LIGHTSABER

LUKE SKYWALKER

OBI-WAN KENOBI

QUEEN AMIDALA

QUI-GON

REBELS

SITH

WOOKIEE

YODA

```
Q I H U K O O D T N U O C
U A D O Y E M P I R E L D
E E S E C D Q I E U O O A
E J A R J A R B I N K S R
N I O A T E A O E C E N T
A F H T I S L N I W E A H
M N E S T V E E O D N H V
I O R H D A R K S I D E A
D G G T Y N S N O G O S D
A I U A K A N A O A R L E
L U K E S K Y W A L K E R
A Q L D W I F I O A R B A
N H U E M N A B N X B E E
D I E E I K O O W Y N R G
O J A B B A T H E H U T T
```

LOST IN NEW YORK

Solve the clues below, and then place the letters in their corresponding spots in the grid to reveal a quote from "Taxi Driver." The letter in the upper-right corner of each grid square refers to the clue the letter comes from. A black square indicates the end of a word.

A. "Taxi Driver" director: 2 wds.

__ __ __ __ __ __ __ __ __ __ __
24 62 80 67 45 3 10 53 68 49 71

__ __ __
34 13 86

B. Travis Bickle's signature haircut

__ __ __ __ __ __
22 2 27 12 61 64

C. Frank, to some

__ __ __ __ __ __
26 4 90 46 6 79

D. He played "Sport": _____ Keitel

__ __ __ __ __ __
41 54 38 73 35 25

E. She played Betsy: 2 wds.

__ __ __ __ __ __ __ __ __ __ __
92 39 47 32 29 5 56 11 23 94 83

__ __ __
70 85 21

F. Anywhere at all

  $\overline{~~~}$ $\overline{~~~}$ $\overline{~~~}$ $\overline{~~~}$ $\overline{~~~}$ $\overline{~~~}$ $\overline{~~~}$ $\overline{~~~}$ $\overline{~~~}$ $\overline{~~~}$ $\overline{~~~}$
  19   78   72   69   84   87   28   81   36   44   55

G. "Taxi Driver" star

  $\overline{~~~}$ $\overline{~~~}$ $\overline{~~~}$ $\overline{~~~}$ $\overline{~~~}$ $\overline{~~~}$
  59   8   88   51   43   18

H. State of complete disorder and chaos

  $\overline{~~~}$ $\overline{~~~}$ $\overline{~~~}$ $\overline{~~~}$ $\overline{~~~}$ $\overline{~~~}$ $\overline{~~~}$ $\overline{~~~}$ $\overline{~~~}$ $\overline{~~~}$ $\overline{~~~}$
  31   93   77   17   30   65   91   7   60   66   50

I. Controversial casting choice: Jodie _____

  $\overline{~~~}$ $\overline{~~~}$ $\overline{~~~}$ $\overline{~~~}$ $\overline{~~~}$ $\overline{~~~}$
  14   15   57   82   95   75

J. Perch relative

  $\overline{~~~}$ $\overline{~~~}$ $\overline{~~~}$ $\overline{~~~}$ $\overline{~~~}$ $\overline{~~~}$ $\overline{~~~}$
  40   48   16   1   74   76   20

K. Major misdeeds

  $\overline{~~~}$ $\overline{~~~}$ $\overline{~~~}$ $\overline{~~~}$ $\overline{~~~}$ $\overline{~~~}$ $\overline{~~~}$ $\overline{~~~}$
  33   37   63   89   52   58   42   9

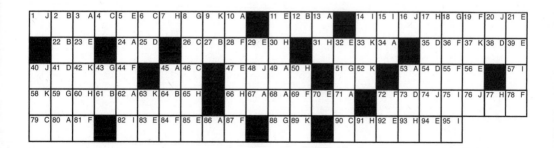

1 J	2 B	3 A	4 C	5 E	6 C	7 H	8 G	9 K	10 A		11 E	12 B	13 A		14 I	15 I	16 J	17 H	18 G	19 F	20 J	21 E
	22 B	23 E		24 A	25 D		26 C	27 B	28 F	29 E	30 H		31 H	32 E	33 K	34 A		35 D	36 F	37 K	38 D	39 E
40 J	41 D	42 K	43 G	44 F		45 A	46 C		47 E	48 J	49 A	50 H		51 G	52 K		53 A	54 D	55 F	56 E		57 I
58 K	59 G	60 H	61 B	62 A	63 K	64 B	65 H		66 H	67 A	68 A	69 F	70 E	71 A		72 F	73 D	74 J	75 I	76 J	77 H	78 F
79 C	80 A	81 F		82 I	83 E	84 F	85 E	86 A	87 F		88 G	89 K		90 C	91 H	92 E	93 H	94 E	95 I

Answers on page 176.

MAHERSHALA ALI MOVIES

ACROSS

1. Auto's wheel bar

5. Xfinity, e.g.: abbr.

8. All-encompassing phrase

12. Balance bar

13. "Me day" destination

14. "Without You" band Mötley ____

15. Advocate strongly

16. Big name in physics

18. Ali was world-class pianist Dr. Don Shirley in this 2018 film

20. A false god

21. 1921 Karel Capek play that introduced the word "robot"

22. Vermont music festival town

25. Health ins. plan

28. Ali was military officer Jim Johnson in this 2016 hit

31. Add-___ (extras)

32. State of inactivity

33. A word from Elsie

35. Prefix meaning eight

36. Ali was Juan, a drug dealer, in this 2016 movie

39. Assumed to be true

41. Gets ready to shoot

44. "I saw ____ kissing Kate..." (tongue twister)

45. "Dune" composer Brian

46. Dubious

47. Biweekly tide

48. "Do not open ____ Xmas"

49. Long-distance swimmer Diana

DOWN

1. Aladdin's monkey

2. Baby Boomer's kid

3. Slowpokes

4. Green gem

5. "Ah, got it"

6. Bit of public relations deception

7. Cook uncovered with no fat

8. Mahershala Ali, for one

9. "Star ____" (Shatner show)

10. "Most assuredly, monsieur!"

11. Branch of Buddhism

17. Coin of little value

19. River through Germany

20. Actor Conrad or actress Barbara

22. Electrical unit now known as a siemens

23. Small planted bulb

24. "Mayberry ____" (old TV show)

25. Make attractive

26. Bit of "dinero"

27. CIA forerunner

29. Mapmaker's subj.

30. Remove shackles

33. Clean the deck

34. Tic-tac-toe win

36. Assigner of G's and R's

37. German director Riefenstahl

38. "Survivor" immunity item

39. China's Sun Yat-____

40. What scuff marks show

42. Advanced music or drama deg.

43. "Danny and the Dinosaur" author ____ Hoff

 Answers on page 177.

BRAT PACK

Change just one letter on each line to go from the top word to the bottom word. Do not change the order of the letters. You must have a common English word at each step.

BRAT

_____ defeat

_____

_____ lease

_____

_____ relative standing

_____

PACK

Answers on page 177.

W_S _ND_RS_N F_LMS

Below is a list of some films Wes Anderson directed. The only thing is, they've lost A, E, I, O, and U, as well as any punctuation and spaces between words. Can you figure out the missing vowels and name each film in the list below?

1. BTTLRCKT

2. THDRJLNGLMTD

3. FNTSTCMRFX

4. THGRNDBDPSTHTL

5. SLFDGS

6. THLFQTCWTHSTVZSS

7. MNRSKNGDM

8. THRYLTNNBMS

9. RSHMR

Answers on page 177.

AMERICA'S "PRETTY WOMAN"

Solve the clues below, and then place the letters in their corresponding spots in the grid to reveal a quote from Julia Roberts. The letter in the upper-right corner of each grid square refers to the clue the letter comes from. A black square indicates the end of a word.

A. Julia's "Pelican Brief" costar

$\overline{}$ $\overline{}$ $\overline{}$ $\overline{}$ $\overline{}$ $\overline{}$
19 66 57 17 36 75

B. 1998 Roberts movie

$\overline{}$ $\overline{}$ $\overline{}$ $\overline{}$ $\overline{}$ $\overline{}$ $\overline{}$
53 23 13 47 35 31 63

C. Julia's "Flatliners" costar (and ex-beau)

$\overline{}$ $\overline{}$ $\overline{}$ $\overline{}$ $\overline{}$ $\overline{}$
10 76 60 33 26 12

D. "Sleeping with _____"

$\overline{}$ $\overline{}$ $\overline{}$ $\overline{}$ $\overline{}$ $\overline{}$ $\overline{}$ $\overline{}$
68 7 48 58 9 18 65 62

E. Kitchen appliances

$\overline{}$ $\overline{}$ $\overline{}$ $\overline{}$ $\overline{}$ $\overline{}$
45 42 72 59 51 29

F. Danny and Rusty in "Ocean's Eleven": 2 wds.

$\overline{}$ $\overline{}$ $\overline{}$ $\overline{}$ $\overline{}$ $\overline{}$ $\overline{}$ $\overline{}$ $\overline{}$
43 49 27 34 21 69 46 39 38

G. Lawyer

41	24	5	54	74	67	78	71

H. Gets along with someone: 3 wds.

40	37	6	50	8	30	56	77	70

I. Actor's tryout

14	73	2	16	44	1	28	4

J. Julia's middle name

32	11	3	55	52

K. Streetwalker

25	22	61	15	64	20

1 I		2 I	3 J	4 I	5 G		6 H	7 D	8 H	9 D	10 C		11 J		12 C	13 B
14 I	15 K	16 I	17 A	18 D	19 A		20 K	21 F	22 K	23 B		24 G	25 K	26 C		27 F
28 I	29 E	30 H		31 B	32 J		33 C	34 F	35 B	36 A		37 H	38 F		39 F	40 H
41 G	42 E		43 F	44 I	45 E		46 F	47 B	48 D	49 F		50 H	51 E	52 J	53 B	54 G
55 J		56 H	57 A		58 D	59 E	60 C	61 K	62 D		63 B	64 K	65 D	66 A	67 G	68 D
	69 F	70 H		71 G	72 E	73 I	74 G		75 A	76 C	77 H	78 G				

Answers on page 177.

BATMEN

ACROSS

1. "Batman Returns" star
8. Sword conqueror
9. Folks on your level
10. Prepare for the future
12. "Isn't ____ bit like you and me?" (Beatles lyric)
13. "The Dark Knight" star
16. Young 'un
18. "Spill it!"
21. In quick succession
23. Burned item
24. "Batman & Robin" star

DOWN

1. Attend to a spill
2. Mythical horseman
3. A as in Athens
4. Spike in movie production
5. Incited to act
6. Kind of fairy
7. Utopia, literally
11. Doolittle created by Shaw
13. Dance, in slang
14. Big bash
15. Leave in the lurch
17. Blood I.D.
19. Try to deceive
20. Like a bubble bath
22. Abbr. in business names

Answers on page 177.

HERE'S TO YOU, MRS. ROBINSON

Cryptograms are messages in substitution code. Break the code to read the movie fact about "The Graduate." For example, THE SMART CAT might be FVO QWGDF JGF if F is substituted for T, V for H, O for E, and so on.

YTPO QFPJADZAQ, BAGXBM

BXRLABR, TQR ITBBXQ GXTMMW

IXBX TDD PAQZFRXBXR LAB MJX

KTBM AL GXQYTNFQ GBTRRAPO

MJTM IXQM MA RVZMFQ JALLNTQ.

Answers on page 177.

CODE-DOKU

Solve this puzzle just like a sudoku. Use deductive logic to complete the grid so that each row, column, and 2 by 3 box contains the letters from the word CINEMA only once.

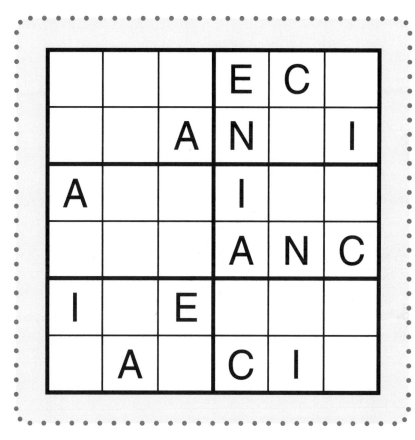

			E	C	
		A	N		I
A			I		
			A	N	C
I		E			
	A		C	I	

Answers on page 178.

SOME OF THE BEST PICTURES

ACROSS

1. Best picture of 1992

7. Dairy case items

8. Beat, as the heart

10. Vital carrier

11. Island of a 1945 battle

12. Current government

14. Submarine sandwich

17. Home for fighter jets

19. Nouveau ____

21. "Sunny" egg parts

22. Prying tool

23. Best picture of 1943

DOWN

1. Felix of "The Odd Couple"

2. Pistol or rifle

3. Enter quickly

4. Performance preceder

5. Loop for a lobe

6. Best picture of 1964

9. Best picture of 1990

13. Big ape

15. Thornton Wilder play

16. Tentatively schedule, with "in"

18. On a cruise, say

20. Deadly snake

Answers on page 178.

FILM STAR

Change just one letter on each line to go from the top word to the bottom word. Do not change the order of the letters. You must have a common English word at each step.

FILM

_____

_____

_____

_____

STAR

Answers on page 178.

HITCHCOCK ANAGRAMS

Unscramble the phrases below to reveal the names of 7 Alfred Hitchcock films.

1. SHY COP

2. RIG VOTE

3. BRED THIS

4. DREAD FILM RUMOR

5. NARRATING SENATORS

6. THROWN SNOTTY HERB

7. WARN WEIRDO

ADDAGRAM

This puzzle functions exactly like an anagram with an added step: In addition to being scrambled, each phrase below is missing the same letter. Discover the missing letter, then unscramble the words. When you do, you'll reveal 4 movies starring Daniel Day-Lewis.

FREAKY GOWNS GO

MORPH THE DATA

ILL CON

A CHEETAH SMOOTHS LIFT

Answers on page 178.

AT THE MOVIES

Every word listed is contained within the group of letters. Words can be found in a straight line horizontally, vertically, or diagonally. They may read either forward or backward.

ACTION	POPCORN
BIG SCREEN	PREVIEWS
CANDY	PROJECTOR
COMEDY	ROMANCE
DIRECTOR	SCENE
DRAMA	SEATS
FEATURE	SHORT
FILM	THEATER
HERO	THRILLER
HORROR	TICKET
MATINEE	VILLAIN
MYSTERY	

```
R Q H A E F U N R O C P O P F Q
T D R E T A E H T G X C A N D Y
Y R I B R E H I R I J S J J F Q
A R O R W O X F R O M A N C E K
P R E H E X Y D E M O C Z Z H X
J L O T S C T N C M E H R S O P
M D Q T S S T Q N A E H L T H R
N B K Q C Y C O V T R O V A H E
E J O W N E M E R I U R J E G V
E R C U I S J C N N T R T S N I
R A C T I O N O T E A O Y I H E
C T H R I L L E R E E R A Z A W
S T H T M B X Z W P F L F L P S
G C L L W P Q X V B L A B Q E M
I Y I K A M A R D I J Y F G Q E
B F H P J G H T V V T I C K E T
```

Answers on page 178.

SAY WHAT?

Below is a group of words that, when properly arranged in the blanks, reveal a quote from John Wayne.

anything motion Westerns closer art picture

_____ are _____ to _____ than _____ else in the _____

_____ business.

UNCONVENTIONAL GENIUS

Cryptograms are messages in substitution code. Break the code to read the movie quote from "Forrest Gump." For example, THE SMART CAT might be FVO QWGDF JGF if F is substituted for T, V for H, O for E, and so on.

"TO TSTTQ QGVQOU UQME

GMRH VQU GMWH Q FSP SR

AXSASGQBHU. OSL DHZHC WDSV

VXQB OSL'CH NSDDQ NHB."

CODE-DOKU

Solve this puzzle just like a sudoku. Use deductive logic to complete the grid so that each row, column, and 2 by 3 box contains the letters from the word ACTORS only once.

C	A			S	
S		O		C	A
T	S		A		R
		R	C	T	S
O	C	A			T
R	T		O	A	

Answers on page 179.

MOVIE REMAKES

ACROSS

1. "A fickle food," per Emily Dickinson
5. "Sesame Street" network
8. PC scrolling key
12. Ancient Egyptians held it sacred
13. Christmas tree sales site
14. 100 cents, in Europe
15. It offers goods under a canvas shelter
17. Apply paint crudely
18. Beyoncé is Nala in this 2019 remake of the first Disney animated film with an original story
20. Barrett of the original Pink Floyd
21. "Cola" lead-in
22. A long way off
25. It means "fire bowl" in Japanese
28. Bill Murray is the voice of Baloo, a good-natured bear, in this 2016 remake of the Kipling tales
32. Repudiate
33. "Amazing Grace" verse ender
34. Chatted with online, briefly
35. "I pity the fool!" speaker

38. Bradley Cooper and Lady Gaga star in this third remake of the 1937 film about an aspiring actress and the actor who helps her (2018)
42. Edmonton's province, briefly
43. Building wing
45. It can get you in on the ground floor
46. Milking parlor sound
47. Body chill
48. Breath mint in a roll, informally
49. "Happy Days" setting
50. Crow's-nest sighting

DOWN

1. Appropriate
2. Act as a getaway driver, say
3. Ho Chi ____ Trail
4. "Blue Bloods" actor Will
5. Bagpiper's pattern
6. Arizona necktie
7. Crate marking, maybe
8. Human-powered taxi
9. Llamas' cousins
10. Controlled substance
11. San Francisco's ____ Hill

16. Admirably crafty

19. Expensive cut of beef

22. Big initials in bouquets

23. Fish wrapped in nori

24. Electric-current blocker

25. "The Time Machine" author's monogram

26. Do groundbreaking work

27. "I Like ____" ('50s campaign slogan)

29. Fruit-filled pastry

30. Eye part that holds the iris

31. Rhyming nickname for Obama

35. Old PC standard

36. A homer provides at least one

37. Add up

38. Succulent with many uses

39. Show that launched Kelly Clarkson's career, familiarly

40. Capital of Latvia

41. "Common" or "proper" word

42. General's assistant: abbr.

44. "Game of Thrones" patriarch

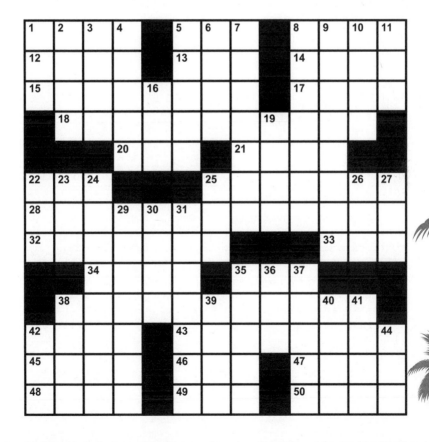

Answers on page 179.

CAN YOU REMAKE THIS REMAKE?

Rearrange the letters in the phrases below to spell the title of a 1991 movie remake (for 1) and the first and last name of one of the film's stars (for 2).

1. HIT FOR FEATHERBED _____

2. VAN TERMITES _____

LETTER TILES

Using the letter tiles, create 10 four-letter words. Create 20, and you're a Word Sleuth; create 30, and you're a Word Wonder; create 40, and you're a Word Master!

T I N S E L T O W N

Answers on page 179.

MAD MAX

Change just one letter on each line to go from the top word to the bottom word. Do not change the order of the letters. You must have a common English word at each step.

FURY

_____ put underground

_____ destroy with fire

_____

_____ affected by wear or use

_____ part of a sentence

_____

_____ place in or on a means of conveyance

ROAD

Answers on page 179.

WHO DIRECTED?

ACROSS

1. "Doggone it!"
5. Cries of insight
9. Atmospheric prefix
10. 53, in old Rome
11. "The Color Purple," 1985. Who directed?
13. ____ podge (mess)
14. "Goldfinger" author Fleming
15. "Chop-chop!"
17. "Anatomy of a Murder," 1959. Who directed?
20. Epoch when mammals emerged
21. Grand Central, e.g.: abbr.
22. Statuette for a star
26. "The Hateful Eight," 2015. Who directed?
28. "Julius Caesar" phrase
29. ____ Domini
30. Clarinetist's mouthpiece
31. Smell like old cigars

DOWN

1. Sprinkle of salt
2. Seized vehicle, informally
3. Sahara-like
4. Reason for a 10th inning, say
5. Edmonton is its cap.
6. Getting a move on
7. Snoopy's flying persona, e.g.
8. John Hancock, notably
12. Make privy to, as a secret
16. Like an awful hotel
17. Be a pain to
18. Perform a pirouette, say
19. Game played with 32 cards
23. French film
24. "Green Gables" girl
25. Castle on a board
27. Embezzler's dread: abbr.

AUDREY ANAGRAMS

Unscramble each phrase below to reveal a film starring Audrey Hepburn.

1. AWAIT TRUNK LID

2. HOLY RADIOMAN

3. A HOT FELINE NONVOTER

4. BANS AIR

5. A FATTY BEARSKIN STAFF

6. THORNY SUNSET

7. FAMILY YARD

8. A HOLLOW TESTIMONIAL

9. AWARD A PENCE

10. CAFE FUNNY

Answers on page 180.

ADDAGRAM

This puzzle functions exactly like an anagram with an added step: In addition to being scrambled, each phrase below is missing the same letter. Discover the missing letter, then unscramble the words. When you do, you'll reveal 4 Jack Nicholson movies.

ABDUCT MOIST

OVERTOOK SWEET CONFLUENCES

DATED PETER

WANT COIN

SAY WHAT?

Below is a group of words that, when properly arranged in the blanks, reveal a quote from early film star Florence Lawrence.

could wonder sit room believe used studio much

dressing making

I _____ to _____ in my _____ _____ at the _____ and _____ just how _____ longer _____ I keep _____ _____.

Answers on page 180.

MATT DAMON MOVIES

ACROSS

1. "Hey there, matey!"

5. "Nightmare" street of film

8. Tennis legend Arthur

12. Perry with a Grammy and five Emmys

13. Aussie marsupial, slangily

14. Growth period

15. Neptune's spears

17. Butter alternative

18. Matt Damon is a NASA astronaut sent to an icy planet in this 2014 sci-fi epic

20. Back muscle, in gym lingo

21. Fox's home

22. "Don't quit your day ___!"

25. Damon is a paroled car thief in another futuristic setting in this 2013 movie

28. "Ah, so sad"

30. Buck's belle

31. Camel feature

32. 2015 finds Damon in yet another sci-fi story in "The ___"

34. "Mad" or "Cosmo," e.g.

35. Very small

36. Dawdle

39. Damon is a European mercenary in this 2016 action monster film from China

44. "Old" British buddy

45. In ___ order (tidy)

46. Boone's nickname

47. Golf ball prop

48. "Blue" or "White" river

49. Fries or slaw, typically

50. "Slippery" swimmer

51. D.C. ball team, briefly

DOWN

1. "Macbeth" opener

2. Auto beeper

3. Do not include

4. Alpine holler

5. Young's partner in accounting

6. Former Mississippi Sen. Trent

7. Light German wine

8. Do away with

9. Sun parlor

10. A gardener, at times

11. Angsty music genre

16. ___ of Good Feelings, 1817–25

19. Deposit, as an egg

22. Ad-lib, musically
23. Ipanema greeting
24. What a shortstop may use to field a grounder
25. 1 billion years, in astronomy
26. "Pulp Fiction" actress Thurman
27. Automobile sticker fig.
29. Church bell spot
30. Certain hotel fee
33. Gerund ending

36. Boutonniere spot
37. Bermuda's ocean: abbr.
38. Oscar winner Edmund of "Miracle on 34th Street"
39. Asian cuisine choice
40. Alternative to saber or foil
41. Capital of Western Samoa
42. Bouncy tune
43. Cask dregs
44. Floppy successors

ACTING ICON

Every word or phrase relating to Jack Nicholson is hidden in the grid. Words can be found in a straight line horizontally, vertically, or diagonally. They may read either forward or backward. Leftover letters will reveal a fact about the actor.

ART COLLECTOR	IRONWEED
ART TALENT	THE JOKER
AS GOOD AS IT GETS	MCMURPHY
CHINATOWN	PRIZZI'S HONOR
CLASS CLOWN	RAGTIME
CUCKOO'S NEST	RANDLE
THE DEPARTED	THE RAVEN
EASY RIDER	REDS
A FEW GOOD MEN	THE WILD RIDE
FIVE EASY PIECES	WOLF
HOFFA	

Leftover Letters: _____

```
N F I V E E A S Y P I E C E S
I C H I N A T O W N C H O L T
D L S O T H E W I L D R I D E
E A N H A S B E E N N O M E G
E S I C U C K O O S N E S T T
W S N A E A S Y R I D E R R I
N C T N E M D O O G W E F A S
O L R O N O H S I Z Z I R P A
R O T C E L L O C T R A E E D
I W E D V F O R A N G F K D O
O N S C A A R I N T L F O E O
M C M U R P H Y I O F O J H G
I V E D E I F M W F E H E T S
R E N T H D E L D N A R H E A
C A A R T T A L E N T D T E S
```

 Answers on page 180.

SC_RS_S_ F_LMS

Below is a list of some films Martin Scorsese directed. The only thing is, they've lost A, E, I, O, and U, as well as any spaces between words. Can you figure out the missing vowels and name each film in the list below?

1. THVTR

2. CSN

3. THCLRFMNY

4. THDPRTD

5. GNGSFNWYRK

6. GDFLLS

7. HG

8. THRSHMN

9. RGNGBLL

10. SHTTRSLND

11. TXDRVR

12. THWLFFWLLSTRT

Answers on page 181.

VIVA HOLLYWOOD!

Move each of the letters below into the grid to form common words. You will use each letter once. The letters in the numbered cells of the grid correspond to the letters in the phrase at the bottom. Completing the grid will help you complete the phrase and vice versa. When finished, the grid and phrase should be filled with valid words, and you will have used all the letters in the letter set.

Hint: The numbered cells in the grid are arranged alphabetically, so the letter in the cell marked 1 will appear in the alphabet before the letter in the cell marked 2, and so on.

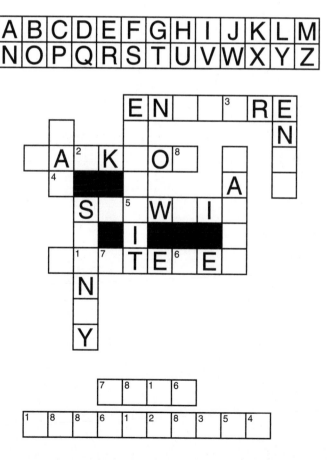

Answers on page 181.

SAOIRSE RONAN MOVIES

ACROSS

1. Fanciful notion

5. "Little Orphan Annie" character (with "The")

8. Bulletin board fastener

12. "King of the road" vagabond

13. British track star Sebastian

14. Bouffant, for one

15. Astra or Vectra maker

16. What the Mohs scale measures

18. Ronan plays Rat in this 2019 dark fairy tale of love and survival

20. Dutch engineering feat

21. "The ___ Couple"

22. Onetime honor for cable TV shows

25. Common Hawaiian dish

28. 2017 fully painted animated feature with Saoirse Ronan as van Gogh's friend Marguerite

31. 180 degrees from WSW

32. Ushered

33. Beginning of a laugh

35. Bonheur or Parks

36. Ronan's character Eleanor Webb is a bloodsucker on the run in this 2012 vampire feature

39. Upper-class wealth

41. Appetizer in Barcelona

44. Animal shelter

45. "Mind the ___" (Underground warning)

46. Administered with a spoon, perhaps

47. 1980s PCs

48. Bard's "before"

49. Abbr. on a food container

DOWN

1. "Horton Hears a ___"

2. "___ on Pop" (Dr. Seuss book)

3. Revival tent cry

4. Island home of Father Damien

5. Berliner's eight

6. Emulate an eagle

7. Kind of table in chemistry class

8. Adjusted guitar strings

9. Copycat

10. Audiophile collection

11. Beats in the ring, for short

17. Netflix delivery

19. Already stitched

20. Brand of bug killer

22. "Game of Thrones" beverage
23. Info on a toy package
24. Campers, briefly
25. Chain with day care
26. ____-day (kind of multivitamin)
27. "____ be a pleasure!" ("Love to!")
29. Seaweed for sushi rolls
30. Caesar salad ingredient
33. Church songs

34. Nitrogen: Prefix
36. Place to sleep in an apt.
37. A stone's throw away
38. A or O, at the blood bank
39. "Mikado" sash
40. Chemist's hangout
42. A hand for Snoopy
43. Key on either side of the space bar

Answers on page 181.

LEADING ACTRESSES

The letters in BAXTER can be found in boxes 6, 7, 8, 11, 17, and 20 but not necessarily in that order. Similarly, the letters in all the other leading actresses' names can be found in the boxes indicated. Your task is to insert all the letters of the alphabet into the boxes. If you do this correctly, the shaded cells will reveal the name of another leading actress.

Hint: Compare SWANK and SWANSON to get the values of K and O, then SWANK and SARANDON for the value of W.

Unused letters: Q, Z

BAXTER: 6, 7, 8, 11, 17, 20

BERGMAN: 3, 6, 8, 13, 15, 17, 20

BURSTYN: 3, 4, 7, 8, 12, 16, 20

DE HAVILLAND: 2, 3, 5, 6, 17, 21, 22, 23

FIELD: 2, 5, 6, 10, 21

HEPBURN: 3, 6, 8, 9, 16, 20, 22

JACKSON: 3, 4, 14, 17, 18, 19, 24

MCDORMAND: 3, 13, 17, 18, 19, 20, 21

SARANDON: 3, 4, 17, 18, 20, 21

SPACEK: 4, 6, 9, 14, 17, 19

STREISAND: 2, 3, 4, 6, 7, 17, 20, 21

SWANK: 1, 3, 4, 14, 17

SWANSON: 1, 3, 4, 17, 18

WYMAN: 1, 3, 12, 13, 17

YOUNG: 3, 12, 15, 16, 18

1	2	3	4	5	6	7	8	9	10	11	12	13

14	15	16	17	18	19	20	21	22	23	24	25	26
											Q	Z

Answers on page 181.

ADDAGRAM

This puzzle functions exactly like an anagram with an added step: In addition to being scrambled, each phrase below is missing the same letter. Discover the missing letter, then unscramble the words. When you do, you'll reveal 4 films from 2019.

AFFORD RIVER

MINI SHEATH

AS DATA

SEVEN GEM AGENDA

BIOPIC

Change just one letter on each line to go from the top word to the bottom word. Do not change the order of the letters. You must have a common English word at each step.

BIO

_____

_____

PIC

Answers on page 181.

LEO IN THE MOVIES

ACROSS

1. Melville's whale hunter

4. Pressed for time

8. 2006 Leonardo DiCaprio film about a gem smuggler

9. Poe's "The ____ Heart"

10. Grown polliwog

11. PR agents concerns

14. Small shake

16. Lipinski leap

18. Flip out

21. 1995 Leonardo DiCaprio movie that is also a lunar event

22. Welcome gesture

23. X, on a greeting card

DOWN

2. Slice in two

3. Lead beside distilled waters?

4. Neighbor of Pakistan

5. Flowering shrubs

6. German sub

7. Bureaucratic excess

12. Fight with the fists

13. Academic type

15. Quick as lightning

17. Spill the beans

19. Bad habits

20. Watering hole

Answers on page 182.

ACROSTIC ANAGRAM

Unscramble the words below, then transfer the corresponding letters to the grid. When you're finished, you'll be rewarded with a quote from Will Rogers. A black square indicates the end of a word.

A. Y   A   Y   N   W   A

___ ___ ___ ___ ___ ___
62   29   68   66   5   10

B. T   C   R   I   A   C

___ ___ ___ ___ ___ ___
67   40   4   30   56   15

C. Y   W   T   E   A   R

___ ___ ___ ___ ___ ___
48   22   14   43   50   59

D. E   W   R   T   O

___ ___ ___ ___ ___
11   39   65   53   46

E. I   C   A   N   H

___ ___ ___ ___ ___
36   12   31   16   42

F. N   Y   A   N   S   O

___ ___ ___ ___ ___ ___
34   6   26   60   54   8

G. Z O E O N
28 21 2 63 37

H. Y I U T I L T
3 23 18 58 20 51 47

I. E D H A E V
52 64 13 33 45 27

J. A N K L F
38 19 49 35 55

K. U O A Y T L
57 9 1 25 61 7

L. D I V V I
44 41 17 24 32

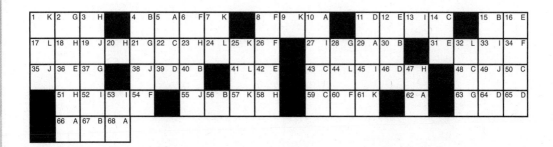

Answers on page 182.

TOM HANKS MOVIES

ACROSS

1. Tom Hanks starred with Meryl Streep in 2017's "The ____"

5. ... playing legendary news paperman ____ Bradlee

8. Allied jumping-off point of July 1944

12. "Cleopatra" river

13. "Hips Don't ____" (2006 Shakira hit)

14. "Hawaii Five-0" star Scott

15. Op-ed artist Pat known for caricatures

17. Comes to the rescue

18. Love letter salutation

19. In a 2016 movie, Hanks touched down successfully as the heroic pilot called "____"

21. Barnyard mama

22. Employs

23. Bunk, e.g.

26. Popular deal-of-the-day website

29. Hanks was New York lawyer James Donovan in this 2015 historical drama

33. Court precedent

34. Rifleman's org.

35. Casual conversation

36. Purely or simply: abbr.

39. Hanks starred with Halle Berry in 2012's science fiction epic, "____ Atlas"

40. Hanks was Eamon ___ in the techno-thriller "The Circle," 2017

44. "Cape ____" (1991 De Niro film)

45. Shapeless

47. 40–30 tennis score, maybe

48. Big name in home dyes

49. "The ____ King" (2019 remake starring Beyoncé)

50. Blue staters, for short

51. Last letter of the Hebrew alphabet, similar to the letter T

52. "Raggedy" dolls

DOWN

1. ____ Penh, Cambodia (Var.)

2. Like a grease monkey's rag

3. Arrived safely under the throw

4. Cheyenne shelter

5. Loud sound from trumpets

6. "Ich Bin ____ Berliner": JFK

7. Browse the web

8. Increase proportionately

9. Out-of-control drop

10. "Luck Be a ___"

11. Add-___ (annexes)

16. "Turn left" command

20. GI hangouts

23. "Dr. Who" network

24. Slice of history

25. Deny

26. Pai ___ (Chinese gambling game)

27. "... ___ the fields we go . . ."

28. Clandestine govt. org.

30. Renders harmless, as a bull

31. Actress Summer of "Firefly"

32. Humbly accept blame

36. "Dancing With the Stars" network

37. Dit's counterpart

38. Cello's smaller cousin

39. Formally hand over

41. Sprawled

42. Bond's alma mater

43. Deep desires

44. "In" thing, for now

46. "My Big Fat Greek Wedding" star Vardalos

Answers on page 182.

ADD-A-WORD

Add one word to each of the 3-word sets to create new words or phrases. For example: In a set including "smith," "fore," and "game," the added word would be "word" (creating "wordsmith," "foreword," and "word game").

1. movie, guest, light: _____

2. film, executive, apartment: _____

3. angle, operator, lens: _____

4. writer, green, big: _____

5. stage, track, diegetic: _____

STILL A HERO

Change just one letter on each line to go from the top word to the bottom word. Do not change the order of the letters. You must have a common English word or a name at each step.

FORD

_____

_____

_____

SOLO

Answers on page 182.

A PUZZLING PERSPECTIVE

Mentally arrange the lettered balls from large to small in the correct order to spell an 11-letter word.

Clue: Factual film

Answer on page 182.

CINEMATOGRAPHERS

Every name listed is contained within the group of letters. Names can be found in a straight line horizontally, vertically, or diagonally. They may read either forward or backward.

ALBERTI (Maryse)

BILL POPE

CONRAD HALL

DESCHANEL (Caleb)

DICK POPE

DION BEEBE

ELSWIT (Robert)

GREGG TOLAND

JOHN SEALE

JOHN TOLL

KAMIŃSKI (Janusz)

KHONDJI (Darius)

LACHMAN (Edward)

LEON SHAMROY

LIBATIQUE (Matthew)

LUBEZKI (Emmanuel)

ŁUKASZ ŻAL

MANDY WALKER

MIRANDA (Claudio)

MORRISON (Rachel)

PRIETO (Rodrigo)

REED MORANO

RICHARDSON (Robert)

ROGER DEAKINS

SANDGREN (Linus)

SPINOTTI (Dante)

STORARO (Vittorio)

VAN HOYTEMA (Hoyte)

WALLY PFISTER

YOUNG (Bradford)

```
E  L  S  W  I  T  E  P  O  P  L  L  I  B  A  D
L  I  B  A  T  I  Q  U  E  K  H  O  N  D  J  I
A  T  K  I  K  S  N  I  M  A  K  B  G  P  R  C
Z  T  W  M  L  L  O  T  N  H  O  J  R  E  I  K
Z  O  W  A  L  L  Y  P  F  I  S  T  E  R  C  P
S  N  G  N  E  A  E  S  N  D  Q  D  G  O  H  O
A  I  M  D  O  H  L  T  M  I  M  E  G  G  A  P
K  P  O  Y  N  D  A  O  I  O  L  S  T  E  R  E
U  S  R  W  S  A  E  R  R  N  U  C  O  R  D  P
L  I  R  A  H  R  S  A  A  B  B  H  L  D  S  R
G  T  I  L  A  N  N  R  N  E  E  A  A  E  O  I
N  R  S  K  M  O  H  O  D  E  Z  N  N  A  N  E
U  E  O  E  R  C  O  A  A  B  K  E  D  K  M  T
O  B  N  R  O  Z  J  S  S  E  I  L  V  I  V  O
Y  L  Z  D  Y  K  A  M  E  T  Y  O  H  N  A  V
L  A  C  H  M  A  N  E  R  G  D  N  A  S  N  W
```

Answers on page 182.

CRYPTOGRAMS

Cryptograms are messages in substitution code. Break the code to read the titles of 10 films starring Gregory Peck. For example, THE SMART CAT might be FVO QWGDF JGF if F is substituted for T, V for H, O for E, and so on. Hint: Look for repeated letters. E, T, A, O, N, R, and I are the most often used letters. A single letter is usually A or I; OF, IS, and IT are common 2-letter words; THE and AND are common 3-letter groups. These cryptograms share a common cipher.

1. CRWKT BRAMNKX

2. YR QMAA K WRSQMTPEMCN

3. YBL PJTU RI TKZKCRTL

4. UGLAAERJTN

5. YBL QLXU RI YBL QMTPNRW

6. PLTYALWKT'U KPCLLWLTY

7. YBL XLKCAMTP

8. YDLAZL R'SARSQ BMPB

9. SKGL ILKC

10. YBL RWLT

Answers on page 183.

DIRECTOR ANAGRAMS

Unscramble each word and phrase to reveal the last names of 14 film directors.

1. EARNS NOD

2. MEN BRAG

3. LOBE WIG

4. TO BURN

5. ROMANCE

6. POLO CAP

7. TOAD WOES

8. HAD ROW

9. O.J. SNACK

10. IN LOCHS

11. SEE CROSS

12. ROB HEDGERS

13. BEEP GIRLS

14. RATION TAN

Answers on page 183.

GRETA GERWIG

ACROSS

1. Got off the ground

5. "A Series of Unfortunate Events" villain Count ____

9. "Chocolate" dog, for short

12. 1969 Creedence Clearwater Revival hit

13. Grow wearisome

14. Hoppy-hour order?

15. Basically alike

16. Faulkner femme fatale ____ Varner

17. Bit of Seurat painting

18. Greta Gerwig is a veterinary nurse in this 2016 dark comedy with Danny DeVito and Julie Delpy

20. "But of course!"

21. "CSI" sample

22. Development site

24. Bug on a plant

27. Authentic

30. Billet-____ (love letter)

31. Bounder

32. "Jurassic Park" character

33. Part mortal and part deity

35. Drops off the grid, say

36. Beehive-raiding beast

37. Any relative

38. Night flyer

40. Gerwig stars in and co-wrote this 2012 comedy directed by companion Noah Baumbach

45. Dish of roasted roots

46. Pate de ____ gras

47. "And others," in lists

48. Flying fish-eater

49. Icelandic literary work

50. Bring down, as a house

51. It gives one good standing?

52. A saxophone has one

53. Bump on a lid

DOWN

1. Diamond defect

2. Mischief-maker of Norse myth

3. "Nurse Jackie" star Falco

4. Southern grocery chain

5. "Einstein on the Beach," for one

6. Give kudos to

7. Gave permission

8. Large wine bottle

9. This 2017 coming-of-age film was nominated for five Oscars, including Best Picture, and Best Director for Greta Gerwig

10. Additive to some soaps

11. Many are placed in Vegas

19. Bring to a conclusion

23. Rebels against Queeg

24. "Just ____ water"

25. "The Bells" writer

26. Greta Gerwig co-stars with Al Pacino in this 2014 comedy-drama (with "The")

27. ____ about (roam)

28. "Her maiden name was" word

29. George Strait's "All My ____ Live in Texas"

31. Eat away at

34. Lighting electrician on a set

35. Involuntary sound

37. Do a bread-making chore

38. Autobahn vehicle

39. Put on, as a uniform

41. Adjutant, e.g.

42. "ER" exclamation

43. Foggy

44. Away from the breeze

Answers on page 183.

ONE TIME

Find the word "movie" once—and only once—in the grid below.

I E I M O V E I
V O V E M M I O
M E M M I E E I
I O M M I V V M
V I V O M V O M
M V I O M I I M
M V M E E O I O
E O E E I E I I

Answer on page 183.

STAR WARS

Change just one letter on each line to go from the top word to the bottom word. Do not change the order of the letters. You must have a common English word at each step.

STAR

———

———

———

———

———

WARS

Answers on page 183.

PARASITE

ACROSS

1. Pitcher plant victim

4. "Parasite" director, producer, and writer: ____ Joon-ho

8. Share some gossip

12. Hawaii's Mauna ____ volcano

13. Flyer to Tel Aviv

14. It means "commander" in Arabic

15. Game lover's purchase

16. Dynamic opener

17. Omar of "House"

18. "Parasite" was Oscar's ____ of 2019

21. Female enlistee in WWII

22. What permissive parents may choose to spare

25. "Faust" character

28. Vets-to-be

29. Number of Disney Dalmatians

30. Pizza joint appliance

31. Party with power

32. Give a long look

33. Beyond the horizon

34. And the rest, briefly

35. Where van Gogh painted "The Night Café"

36. Philadelphia hockey team

38. New Deal agcy. of 1933

39. "Parasite" won four major Oscars, including one for "Best International ____"

44. Ump's ruling

46. Campsite visitor

47. Take-home item

48. Type of bond, for short

49. Slangy turnarounds

50. Colony member

51. Arcade game ____-Ball

52. State of comfort

53. Dit's counterpart in Morse code

DOWN

1. Toning target

2. Wolf's gait

3. Barks sharply

4. "Help me out here, bud"

5. Olive oil's ____ acid

6. Sting figure

7. Opening between the vocal cords

8. Big name in tractors and such

9. Bygone Chrysler

10. Drink sample

11. Slugger's stat
19. Sealy choice
20. Nervous speaker's sounds
23. Leak out slowly
24. Breaks down
25. Tip, as one's derby
26. Feedback for a prof.
27. Nearly mint, to a collector
28. Big chain in health supplements
31. "I'm not making it up!"
32. Rival of Seles

34. The Mesozoic, e.g.
35. Reluctant
37. Causing chills, maybe
38. They beat twos
40. Iris container
41. Apple store purchase
42. Clark's crush
43. Legend
44. Most NPR stations
45. Puffin, e.g.

Answers on page 183.

CASABLANCA QUOTES

Cryptograms are messages in substitution code. Break the code to read the famous quotes from *Casablanca*. For example, THE SMART CAT might be FVO QWGDF JGF if F is substituted for T, V for H, O for E, and so on. Hint: Look for repeated letters. E, T, A, O, N, R, and I are the most often used letters. The code is the same for all six quotes.

1. "JWBW'U IZZMSTD NX HZL, MSG."

2. "IZLSU, S XJSTM XJSU SU XJW RWDSTTSTD ZP N RWNLXSPLI PBSWTGUJSC."

3. "ZP NII XJW DST EZSTXU ST NII XJW XZVTU ST NII XJW VZBIG, UJW VNIMU STXZ ASTW."

4. "CINH SX, UNA. CINH 'NU XSAW DZWU RH.'"

5. "BZLTG LC XJW LULNI ULUCWKXU."

6. "VW'II NIVNHU JNFW CNBSU."

CODE-DOKU

Solve this puzzle just as you would a sudoku. Use deductive logic to complete the grid so that each row, column, and 3 by 3 box contains the letters from the words FUN MOVIES.

		S	N	U	E			
		M	F					
F		E				S		
				O	M			F
V	N						S	I
M			I	N				
		V				O		M
					U	E		
			S	M	N	I		

Answers on page 184.

THE ORDINARY HERO

ACROSS

1. Disney's football-kicking mule

4. Shindig

8. 1980s TV sheriff

12. "Tokyo Story" director Yasujiro

13. Barbara in "Voyage to the Bottom of the Sea"

14. First name in daredeviltry

15. Assault on the ears

16. Jimmy Stewart's wife in "It's a Wonderful Life"

18. Martin Sheen, to Charlie

20. Mr. Moto portrayer Peter

21. Jimmy Stewart's girlfriend in "Rear Window"

26. Actress Skye

27. Yale grads

28. CFO's degree

31. "Peanuts" fussbudget

32. Adverse

33. Kennel cry

34. Dismiss summarily

35. German trio

36. Fencing sword

37. Jimmy Stewart's assistant in "Mr. Smith Goes to Washington"

39. Fur capitalist John Jacob

42. Number for the second sequel

43. Jimmy Stewart's wife in "The Man Who Shot Liberty Valance"

47. Health club

50. 2000 title role for Julia

51. It has a crest and a trough

52. Greek letter

53. Emulates Eminem

54. The yoke's on them

55. Mork's home planet

DOWN

1. Morgan Freeman's role in "Bruce Almighty"

2. Terrorist's weapon in movies

3. "Butch Cassidy and the ____ Kid"

4. Actor Watanabe in "Sixteen Candles"

5. Tumult

6. Broadway actor Cariou

7. "Scarface" actress Dvorak

8. Loretta Lockhorn's hubby, in the comics

9. Song from "The Wizard of Oz," "____ the Rainbow"

10. Bar suds

11. Ye ____ Tea Shoppe

17. "____ right with the world"

19. ____-deucy

21. Monster lizard

22. Sauce thickener

23. "Pride & Prejudice" star Knightley

24. Talk show host DeGeneres

25. "Lilies of the Field" costar Skala

28. 1981 Klaus Maria Brandauer film

29. ____ cheese dressing

30. One who imitates

33. Himalayan beast in "The Mummy: Tomb of the Dragon Emperor"

35. Skin suffix

37. Crawford and Blondell

38. Ascended

39. Declare with confidence

40. End of Doris Day's theme song

41. Press junket

44. ____ Jima

45. Not strict

46. Actress Arden in "Anatomy of a Murder"

48. 72 at Pebble Beach, e.g.

49. Diving seabird

Answers on page 184.

BASEBALL ANAGRAMS

Unscramble the phrases below to reveal the titles of 9 baseball movies.

1. ONLY BLAME

2. HEAL TRUANT

3. AFFORDED SMILE

4. HANDLE TOTS

5. ELEVATE MOTHER OFF HOG

6. FEATURE A WOOL HINGE

7. AREA MULE JOG

8. HOOKER TIE

9. THEME OUTING

Answers on page 184.

LETTER TILES

Using the letter tiles, create 10 five-letter words. Create 20, and you're a Word Sleuth; create 30, and you're a Word Wonder; create 40, and you're a Word Master!

S C R E E N P L A Y

ADDAGRAM

This puzzle functions exactly like an anagram with an added step: In addition to being scrambled, each phrase below is missing the same letter. Discover the missing letter, then unscramble the words. When you do, you'll reveal 4 films starring Amy Adams.

ALIENATES CHUM

SEAT THEM

ALMANAC NOUN LIST

A VIRAL

Answers on page 184.

THE PRINCESS BRIDE

Answer each question. Then search for the answers you supplied within the group of letters. Words can be found in a straight line horizontally, vertically, or diagonally. They may read either forward or backward.

1. The iconic movie came out in this year. _____

2. It was based on a novel by this writer. _____

3. The novel was published in this year. _____

4. Buttercup lives in this country. _____

5. The farmhand played by Cary Elwes is named: _____

6. Vizzini is played by this actor. _____

7. Robin Wright, who played Buttercup, played General _____ in "Wonder Woman."

8. Humperdinck wants to frame this country for Buttercup's death. _____

9. This actor played Count Rugen, the six-fingered man. _____

10. This was the name of Miracle Max's wife, played by Carol Kane. _____

11. The Cliffs of Insanity are in reality the Cliffs of _____ in Ireland.

12. Vizzini's famous word. _____

13. The role of the Impressive Clergyman was played by this actor. _____

14. The Man in Black tells Inigo Montoya to get used to this.

_____

15. Inigo's father's first name was this. _____

```
T  A  E  T  R  M  H  C  I  T  F  J  W  N  Y  3  E
S  I  V  F  D  W  X  W  P  B  D  M  W  M  7  L  N
E  A  N  T  I  O  P  E  G  V  P  A  M  9  B  D  A
U  G  U  I  L  D  E  R  Z  K  H  V  1  A  F  I  M
G  W  E  S  T  L  E  Y  O  S  O  U  V  X  L  S  D
R  M  P  D  G  M  U  O  E  C  C  I  F  E  O  A  L
E  A  C  L  V  R  C  C  H  L  E  J  I  U  R  P  O
H  D  W  W  D  R  A  C  H  C  E  I  S  V  I  P  G
P  E  B  W  E  L  L  W  N  Y  J  X  J  A  N  O  M
O  A  Z  T  L  E  Q  O  C  F  M  F  L  L  H  I  A
T  W  E  A  Q  C  C  W  N  W  D  O  X  E  Q  N  I
S  P  W  C  Y  N  V  Q  W  C  O  G  E  R  L  T  L
I  S  T  W  I  R  D  1  K  E  I  N  Q  I  R  M  L
R  B  K  M  X  P  Y  T  9  J  Q  I  G  E  A  E  I
H  X  J  I  A  P  Z  L  O  8  B  M  H  P  D  N  W
C  B  Y  Q  L  T  T  W  P  Q  7  O  I  N  A  T  V
R  L  I  P  I  T  C  L  L  G  M  D  P  I  G  T  H
```

Answers on page 185.

BEST DAY EVER

Cryptograms are messages in substitution code. Break the code to read the movie fact. For example, THE SMART CAT might be FVO QWGDF JGF if F is substituted for T, V for H, O for E, and so on.

DYPWQSKPD SIE AIU QPC TVMFOS VQ

HWQJUWCIAQOE, HOQQUEMZIQVI,

RWC VQ APPSUCPGX, VMMVQPVU.

RVMM FWYYIE AIU RVCCOQ RE CKO

DYPWQSKPD CAVGO SWYVQD

UKPPCVQD.

QUOTE JUMBLE

Unscramble the well-known quote from Will Rogers.

"To somebody happens everything else

long is as funny as it."

Answers on page 185.

CODE-DOKU

Solve this puzzle just like a sudoku. Use deductive logic to complete the grid so that each row, column, and 3 by 3 box contains the letters from the film title FIGHT CLUB only once.

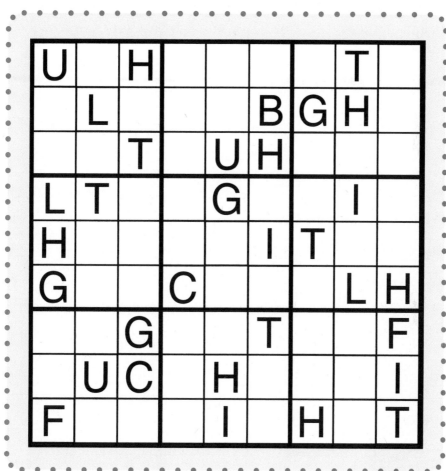

Answers on page 185.

BEST PICTURE ANAGRAMS

Every word or phrase listed is an anagram of a film title that won the Best Picture Oscar. The year it won is listed in parentheses. First, unscramble the letters to figure out the title, then search for it in the grid. Titles can be found in a straight line horizontally, vertically, or diagonally. They may read either forward or backward.

1. A FORBEARANCE WAIL (1962)

2. ASPIRATE (2019)

3. AVERT REHAB (1995)

4. BODY COMING WITH (1969)

5. BROKEN EGO (2018)

6. CASABA CLAN (1943)

7. CHARS (2005)

8. CLEANSED WITH VOWS (1990)

9. DRILLS SNITCHES (1993)

10. FORGETS RUMP (1994)

11. FORGIVE NUN (1992)

12. GOT RADIAL (2000)

13. HER OFFICIATORS (1981)

14. HINT GLOOM (2016)

15. IN ATTIC (1997)

16. LEAPED ON PRIORY (1980)

17. LIGHT POST (2015)

18. MAIN RAN (1988)

19. RUB HEN (1959)

20. SEPARATE HEFT HOW? (2017)

21. SKETCHING SHEEP (2010)

22. THEE THUNDERER (1978)

23. VALUABLE TO (1950)

```
O D T S I L S R E L D N I H C S A
K A K H C E E P S S G N I K E H T
T N O R D I N A R Y P E O P L E G
H C O D N B A T H G I L N O O M O
E E B H A C A S A B L A N C A N B
S S N N T R G L A D I A T O R D G
H W E E I A L P L G C I N A T I T
A I E B M S L R P A R A S I T E N
P T R A E H E V A R B E N H U R H
E H G E R I F F O S T O I R A H C
O W U N F O R G I V E N U F T I O
F O R R E S T G U M P L N T L D P
W L S K R E T N U H R E E D E H T
A V A W N S P O T L I G H T D V R
T E R M N I A R R A I N M A N I E
E S C Y O B W O C T H G I N D I M
R A I B A R A F O E C N E R W A L
```

Answers on page 185.

ELEVATOR WORDS

Like an elevator, words move up and down the "floors" of this puzzle. Starting with the first answer, the second part of each answer carries down to become the first part of the following answer. With the clues given, complete the puzzle.

1. Men In _____

2. _____ _____

3. _____ _____

4. _____ _____

5. _____

6. _____ _____

7. _____smith

1. Tommy Lee Jones-Will Smith sci-fi film series

2. 2010 movie starring Natalie Portman

3. Ballet being performed in the movie above

4. 2006 Sandra Bullock-Keanu Reeves romance, with "The"

5. Like a pet that's trained to go to the bathroom outside

6. 1996 movie starring John Travolta and Christian Slater

7. 1931 film adapted from a Sinclair Lewis novel

 Answers on page 186.

OCEAN'S ELEVEN ANAGRAMS

Unscramble the phrases below to reveal the names of 10 actors in the film "Ocean's Eleven."

1. ENCORE GEOLOGY

2. BAT DRIPT

3. MADMAN TOT

4. A SULTRIER JOB

5. LINER RACER

6. GLUED LIT TOOL

7. SLY FACE CAKES

8. A CANARY DIG

9. BRACE MINE

10. AS CONTACT

Answers on page 186.

FRANCES MCDORMAND FILMS

ACROSS

1. Bread fit for gyros

5. "Minnesota" pool pro

9. Bug for payment

12. "Right on, preacher"

13. Arches National Park state

14. "Now ____ heard everything!"

15. Give an edge to

16. "Cubic" Rubik

17. Aral or Caspian

18. After losing everything in the recession, Fern (Frances McDormand) joins real-life nomads exploring the American West in this 2020 film

20. Bit of butter

21. Aides for MDs

22. Classic Icelandic poetry

24. Animal support org.

27. Response to "Would I look good in this?"

30. Act as usher

31. "Masterpiece" airer

32. Bad marks for a teen

33. Not kidding

35. High priest's garment

36. Eight, to Hans und Franz

37. "Right, skipper"

38. It's not much

40. McDormand won a Best Actress Oscar for her portrayal of Minnesota police chief Marge ____ in 1996's "Fargo"

45. "Boola Boola" collegian

46. Foil's duller relative

47. Cloud of gloom

48. "Gilligan's Island" signal

49. "And others," briefly

50. Busy doing nothing

51. Spot for a first shot

52. "J'accuse" author Emile

53. Cheek by jowl

DOWN

1. Chess "soldier"

2. "As I see it" online

3. Abound

4. South Pole region

5. Coal and oil, for two

6. Old Gillette razor model

7. Hide workers

8. Of inferior quality

9. McDormand is a journalist profiling student revolutionaries in this 2020 film, "The French ____"

10. Colorful eye part

11. Like Felix, but not Oscar

19. "The Double Helix" subject

23. It's not needed with Huggies

24. "Kick-____" (2010 superhero movie)

25. "Catch my drift?"

26. McDormand plays the brash Dr. Verstak in 1997's fact-based Australian war film, "____ Road"

27. "The Superstation"

28. Tokyo-born Grammy winner

29. "Deliverance" actor Beatty

31. Encouraged in mischief

34. "That's awkward"

35. Aperture of a needle

37. "A Passage to India" woman ____ Quested

38. Audition, for instance

39. Soothing botanical

41. "Hud" Oscar-winner Patricia

42. "Smooth Operator" singer

43. Big earthenware jar

44. Brave or Giant, slangily

127   *Answers on page 186.*

BLACK PANTHER

Every word listed is contained within the group of letters. Words can be found in a straight line horizontally, vertically, or diagonally. They may read either forward or backward.

BORDER TRIBE	OKOYE
CHADWICK BOSEMAN	RAMONDA
DANAI GURIRA	RHINOCEROS
DORA MILAJE	RIVER TRIBE
ERIK STEVENS	RYAN COOGLER
EVERETT ROSS	SHURI
HEART-SHAPED HERB	T'CHAKA
JABARI	T'CHALLA
KILLMONGER	ULYSSES KLAUE
LUPITA NYONG'O	VIBRANIUM
M'BAKU	WAKANDA
MICHAEL B. JORDAN	WAR DOG
NAKIA	W'KABI
N'JADAKA	ZURI
N'JOBU	

```
R H I N O C E R O S A E O Z M N L Z A
J C I Z N V B O R D E R T R I B E O K
N H E U J G S R N F E K D E M H P J A
A A S M O S S O R T T E R E V E I D D
D D Z U B Q M Z R E V F G G A A L O A
R W A I U A W F E B M U R P X R E R J
O I V N R L R F C I E L E K N T F A N
J C A A A N E D X R R Y G O X S Q M O
B K L R D I L M Z T Y S N P Z H B I G
L B L B X A G X J R D S O S H A E L N
E O A I A D O U X E S E M E K P A A O
A S H V Y N O S R V D S L U O E K J Y
H E C Y Z A C V Z I H K L C M D A E N
C M T P E K N S K R R L I U N H H V A
I A R Y T A A A H I B A K W N E C I T
M N O T D W Y S K U W U C T B R T Z I
F K J A B A R I B I R E R X W B U A P
O L K I G S W X J W A I G O D R A W U
J Y V E H B S N E V E T S K I R E X L
```

Answers on page 186.

C_ _N BR_TH_RS

Below is a list of some of the films directed by the Coen brothers. The only thing is, they've lost A, E, I, O, and U, as well as any punctuation and spaces between words. Can you figure out the missing vowels and name each film in the list below?

1. THBLLDFSTRSCRGGS

2. BRTNFNK

3. THBGLBWSK

4. BLDSMPL

5. BRDGFSPS

6. BRNFTRRDNG

7. FRG

8. GMBT

9. THHDSCKRPRXY

10. NSDLLWYNDVS

11. NTLRBLCRLTY

12. THLDYKLLRS

13. NCNTRYFRLDMN

14. BRTHRWHRRTTH

15. RSNGRZN

16. SRSMN

17. SBRBCN

18. TRGRT

Answers on page 187.

LETTER TILES

Using the letter tiles, create 10 five-letter words. Create 20, and you're a Word Sleuth; create 30, and you're a Word Wonder; create 40, and you're a Word Master!

C I N E M A T O G R A P H E R

SAY WHAT?

Below is a group of words that, when properly arranged in the blanks, reveal a quote from Daniel Day-Lewis.

somebody developed problem suppose believe

self-delusion highly

I _____ I have a _____ _____ capacity for _____, so it's

no _____ for me to _____ I'm _____ else.

Answers on page 187.

MERYL STREEP MOVIES

ACROSS

1. Comfy footwear, for short
5. "What, me worry?" magazine
8. Film-rating grp.
12. Brief brouhaha
13. Bar brew, briefly
14. "A Farewell to ____" (Hemingway)
15. One's 'hood, for short
16. "That's life!"
18. Tommy Lee Jones and Steve Carell co-starred with Streep in this 2012 romantic comedy-drama
20. "Animal Farm" setting
21. Belgian 1914 battle river
22. "Thriller" follow-up
25. Playwright Stoppard
27. Bite-size appetizer
30. Streep plays vacationing housewife Ellen Martin in this 2019 biographical comedy-drama with Gary Oldman and Antonio Banderas
34. "The Kitchen God's ____"
35. Comstock find
36. "Jeanne d'Arc," for one: abbr.
37. Extremely narrow shoe marking
40. "Goody Two Shoes" singer Adam
42. Streep is British activist Emmeline Pankhurst in this 2015 historical drama
46. Comfortably off
47. Burden
49. "Aphrodite" sculptor
50. "____ Wiedersehen" (goodbye)
51. 100 percent, as gold
52. It's right on a map?
53. Basketball official
54. Do a stevedore's job

DOWN

1. Bill Gates's ISP
2. Aquarium beauty
3. Baja resort area, familiarly
4. "The 39 ____" (Hitchcock movie)
5. Love-letter signoff
6. Each, informally
7. Cheese farm
8. Small electric generator
9. Theatrical handouts
10. "My Cup Runneth Over" singer
11. Donkey or burro relative

17. "Whether _____ nobler in the mind to suffer…": Hamlet

19. "At Last" singer James

22. "Incidentally" in a chat room

23. Fish on a sushi menu

24. Fails to pay back, as a loan

26. 6 on a phone pad

28. "Heartbreaker" singer Benatar

29. Grabbed a bite

31. Candidate's handout

32. Carry away

33. "The Pilgrim" painter Magritte

38. At the back of the boat

39. Bustling with noise or excitement

41. Alternatives to moonroofs

42. "Buona _____" (Italian "Good evening")

43. In unison, musically

44. Carpenter's fastener

45. 100 cents, in Europe

46. Easy to miss

48. Attach a patch, say

1	2	3	4		5	6	7		8	9	10	11
12					13				14			
15					16		17					
	18			19								
			20				21					
22	23	24		25		26			27		28	29
30			31				32	33				
34					35				36			
		37		38	39		40		41			
	42					43				44	45	
46								47			48	
49					50			51				
52					53			54				

Answers on page 187.

A DAME WHO WAS ONCE *THE QUEEN*

Cryptograms are messages in substitution code. Break the code to read the quote from Helen Mirren. For example, THE SMART CAT might become FVO QWGDF JGF if F is substituted for T, V for H, O for E, and so on.

"QEIB SZW RZ METVIMXITKI, GEIS

GEOBV SZW NWMG DI OBGIAAOFIBG

DILTWMI GEIS GEOBV SZW

WBRIKMGTBR QETG SZW'KI MTSOBF."

ADDAGRAM

This puzzle functions exactly like an anagram with an added step: In addition to being scrambled, each word or phrase below is missing the same letter. Discover the missing letter, then unscramble the words. When you do, you'll reveal 4 movies from 2019.

I'LL MEET NOW   INVOKE US

OARS ARE GRIMY   SPIREA

Answers on page 187.

BIG SCREEN LETTERBOX

The letters in MARX can be found in boxes 1, 2, 11, and 20, but not necessarily in that order. The same is true for the other actors' names listed below. Using the names and the box numbers that follow them to guide you, insert all the letters of the alphabet into the boxes. If you do this correctly, the shaded cells will reveal 2 more film stars.

BULLOCK: 6, 7, 15, 19, 21, 26

CLIFT: 7, 8, 13, 16, 19

DE NIRO: 3, 6, 8, 9, 20, 24

GIBSON: 3, 4, 6, 8, 15, 18

JACKSON: 3, 4, 5, 6, 11, 19, 26

KIDMAN: 1, 3, 8, 11, 24, 26

MARX: 1, 2, 11, 20

McQUEEN: 1, 3, 9, 19, 21, 25

PACINO: 3, 6, 8, 11, 17, 19

SCHWARZENEGGER: 3, 4, 9, 11, 12, 18, 19, 20, 22, 23

SMITH: 1, 4, 8, 16, 23

VALENTINO: 3, 6, 7, 8, 9, 10, 11, 16

WAYNE: 3, 9, 11, 12, 14

1	2	3	4	5	6	7	8	9	10	11	12	13

14	15	16	17	18	19	20	21	22	23	24	25	26

Answers on page 188.

NOT A HACK

Every word listed is contained within the group of letters. Words can be found in a straight line horizontally, vertically, or diagonally. They may read either forward or backward. Leftover letters reveal a fact about Gene Hackman.

ABSOLUTE POWER	HEIST
ANOTHER WOMAN	HOOSIERS
ANTZ	LEX LUTHOR
BEHIND ENEMY LINES	THE MEXICAN
BITE THE BULLET	MISUNDERSTOOD
THE CHAMBER	NO WAY OUT
CLASS ACTION	POWER
THE CONVERSATION	PRIME CUT
CRIMSON TIDE	REDS
ENEMY OF THE STATE	RIOT
EUREKA	TARGET
EXTREME MEASURES	TWILIGHT
THE FIRM	UNFORGIVEN
GET SHORTY	WYATT EARP

```
H M I S U N D E R S T O O D E W O
N S A N N Y T R O H S T E G O S R
C E A R F F T O E A E A R B H I E
W N S R O O H M C N R R L I E U W
Y I A S R J E I R O U G M T R N O
A L M Y G X C I I T S E R E W O P
T Y P O I P O E M H A T K T R W E
T M Y C V T N M S E E A E H E A T
E E A D E H V R O R M N P E B Y U
A N O Y N G E I N W E T R B M O L
R E D S L I R F T O M Z I U A U O
P D E I S L S E I M E N M L H T S
T N H O E I A H D A R F E L C R B
E I O N C W T T E N T H C E E C A
O H E I S T I N L E X L U T H O R
N E N E M Y O F T H E S T A T E E
C B T I O N N O I T C A S S A L C
```

Answers on page 188.

RHYME TIME

Each clue leads to a 2-word answer that rhymes, such as BIG PIG or STABLE TABLE. The numbers in parentheses after the clue give the number of letters in each word. For example, "cookware taken from the oven (3, 3)" would be "hot pot."

1. Great film, in hippy parlance (6, 5): _____

2. Harm Astaire's dance partner Rogers (6, 6):

   _____

3. Sees Tom in "Mission: Impossible" (5, 6): _____

4. Snapshot of Dorothy's dog (4, 5): _____

5. Test on Ms. Taylor (3, 4): _____

6. Let actor Brad in (5, 4): _____

7. Lone part in movie (4, 4): _____

8. Goad actress Winslet (4, 4): _____

Answers on page 188.

FILM CREW

Change just one letter on each line to go from the top word to the bottom word. Do not change the order of the letters. You must have a common English word at each step.

FILM

_____

_____

_____

_____ courageous act

_____

_____ defect

_____

_____ shine

_____

_____

CREW

Answers on page 188.

NOT EXACTLY A "MAN WITH NO NAME"

Every word listed is contained within the group of letters. Words can be found in a straight line horizontally, vertically, or diagonally. They may read either forward or backward. Leftover letters reveal a fact about Clint Eastwood.

ALISON	MAYOR
BLOOD WORK	MYSTIC RIVER
BRONCO BILLY	PALE RIDER
CARMEL	PINK CADILLAC
CHANGELING	PREACHER
CITY HEAT	RAWHIDE
DIRECTOR	SONDRA LOCKE
DIRTY HARRY	SUDDEN IMPACT
EIGER SANCTION	TEHAMA
HONKYTONK MAN	THE DEAD POOL
JOE KIDD	TIGHTROPE
MAKE MY DAY	

Leftover Letters: _____

```
C P I N K C A D I L L A C L L
I R N A S O N D R A L O C K E
S E T M N B E P A R O S H B M
U A T K O L R A W E O Y A R R
D C O N I O O L O V P R N O A
D H D O T O T E I I D R G N C
E E N T C D C R S R A A E C A
N R O Y N W E I D C E H L O N
I O S K A O R D A I D Y I B N
M Y I N S R I E A T E T N I G
P A L O R K D R R S H R G L A
A M A H E T A E H Y T I C L M
C O F O G M A K E M Y D A Y O
T L J T I G H T R O P E D W E
S T A C E D I H W A R T I O N
```

Answers on page 188.

SAY WHAT?

Below is a group of words that, when properly arranged in the blanks, reveal a quote from James Stewart.

clean triumph simple picture adhere underdog

involve rules them bully have inflexible ingredients

I _____ my own _____ and _____ to _____. The rule is _____ but _____. A James Stewart _____ must have two vital _____: it will be _____ and it will _____ the _____ of the _____ over the _____.

Answers on page 188.

BOND ANAGRAMS

Unscramble each word or phrase below to reveal a Bond film.

1. A FORMER DEAD VERSION

2. IT WOKE VILLA

3. A NOISY ORACLE

4. FIND LOGGER

5. DONATE HAYRIDE

6. ELEGY DONE

7. INVALID DELETE

8. RANK ROMEO

9. EDIT EMOTION

10. FAMOUS CLAN QUOTE

11. SLY FLAK

12. HALT BLUNDER

13. RESPECT

14. DEATH'S NIGHTLY VIGIL

15. OVERTIRED NEWSROOM

Answers on page 189.

"SHE DID IT THE HARD WAY"

ACROSS

1. Amo, amas, ____
5. Outlawed spray
8. Shells, e.g.
12. Speed Racer's car
14. Seven-day period
15. 1956 Bette Davis film, with "The"
17. Order between "ready" and "go"
18. Lindley of "The Ropers"
19. Moisten the turkey
22. Campus place
24. Largest continent
25. Disadvantages
26. Trygve's successor
29. Davis role in "Now, Voyager"
32. Modeling line?
33. Currier's partner
34. Golfer's club choice
35. TV music marketer
36. ____ Foods, maker of Little Debbie cakes
37. Tati's "ta ta"
40. Collapsible bed
41. Movie in which Davis played Catherine the Great
47. Middle Eastern sultanate
48. Things to be proven
49. Hair quality
50. It's heard before "gee"
51. "Thank ____ Lucky Stars" (1943 all-star musical that included Davis)

DOWN

1. Cable channel for film devotees
2. Cry of farm young
3. Play a role
4. 1952 Bette Davis film
5. Go easy on the calories
6. Netflix rental
7. Afternoon drink
8. Terrible
9. Anthrolopogist Margaret
10. Prime Minister elected in March 1969
11. Cajun staple
13. Let loose
16. Fake
19. One of the Three B's
20. ____ Stadium in Queens
21. Land of Chang and Eng

22. Davis starred in the pilot for this TV series

23. Colonial critters?

25. Shoreline recess

26. 1939 Davis melodrama, with 31-Down

27. Skin lotion ingredient

28. Hackman of "Unforgiven"

30. Started smoking

31. See 26-Down

35. Oft-killed "South Park" character

36. Magic charm

37. "Get ____" (1958 hit song)

38. Major ending

39. "It made me sick when ____ to let ya kiss me": Davis in "Of Human Bondage"

40. Bass, for one

42. Gave in to the munchies

43. 14 and up, for short

44. Hero of "The Matrix" trilogy

45. Down Under bird

46. Kazakhstan, once: abbr.

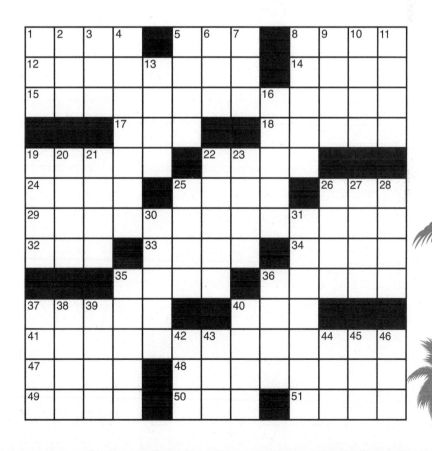

Answers on page 189.

LIGHTS, CAMERA, ACTION!

Every word listed is contained within the group of letters. Words can be found in a straight line horizontally, vertically, or diagonally. They may read either forward or backward.

ACTION	ENSEMBLE	ROLE
ACTOR	FILM	SCENE
AUDITION	INTERVIEW	SCREEN TEST
BIT	LIGHTS	SCRIPT
CAMEO	LINES	SET
CAMERA	LOCATION	STAR
CAST	MEMORIZE	TABLE READ
CHARACTER	PART	TAKE
CREDIT	PLAY	TITLE
DEBUT	PREMIERE	
DIALOGUE	REHEARSE	

```
D B T R E H E A R F N T R A P
D E L I G H K R I R O M E M K
R T B C D S A E Y L I G H T S
O I S U A E T M I N T E R V I
L T B E T S R A I R C S S S T
E L N U R E T C A R A H C T C
N E O G B I T U P L A Y R A A
I L I O C P D E R E I M E R P
L B T L L I E Z I R O M E M C
R M A A T W E I V R E T N I A
O E C I D A E R E L B A T E M
T S O D B I E S R A E H E R E
C N L I N E S T P I R C S S O
A E E M A C S C E N E M T E R
L O R F I L M S C R E E N T E
```

Answers on page 189.

LOVE OR MONEY

Solve the clues below, and then place the letters in their corresponding spots in the grid to reveal a quote from "Slumdog Millionaire." The letter in the upper-right corner of each grid square refers to the clue the letter comes from. A black square indicates the end of a word.

A. Director of "Slumdog Millionaire": 2 wds.

___ ___ ___ ___ ___ ___ ___ ___ ___ ___
50 48 51 68 72 81 14 91 76 19

B. Hard to _____

___ ___ ___ ___ ___ ___ ___
9   16 67 43 75 6   53

C. "Who Wants to Be a Millionaire," for example: 2 wds.

___ ___ ___ ___ ___ ___
65 78 47 70 38 73

D. Oblivious

___ ___ ___ ___ ___ ___ ___
56 49 90 83 1   80 71

E. Anthony Dod Mantle's part in the film

___ ___ ___ ___ ___ ___ ___ ___ ___ ___
61 34 12 32 3   52 20 18 28 36 66

___ ___
82 93

F. Pivotal point

___ ___ ___ ___ ___
37 21 39 11 40

G. Quiz show fodder

$\overline{}$ $\overline{}$ $\overline{}$ $\overline{}$ $\overline{}$ $\overline{}$
33   8   60   22   74   45

H. Uncanny

$\overline{}$ $\overline{}$ $\overline{}$ $\overline{}$ $\overline{}$
58   79   59   23   35

I. Emotional anguish

$\overline{}$ $\overline{}$ $\overline{}$ $\overline{}$ $\overline{}$ $\overline{}$ $\overline{}$ $\overline{}$ $\overline{}$
5   63   87   57   69   85   26   27   92

J. Like the game show host, sometimes

$\overline{}$ $\overline{}$ $\overline{}$ $\overline{}$ $\overline{}$ $\overline{}$ $\overline{}$
84   42   15   25   46   86   54

K. Trailblazer

$\overline{}$ $\overline{}$ $\overline{}$ $\overline{}$ $\overline{}$ $\overline{}$ $\overline{}$
88   29   31   24   77   17   64

L. Roll around, as in mud

$\overline{}$ $\overline{}$ $\overline{}$ $\overline{}$ $\overline{}$ $\overline{}$
4   10   44   89   55   41

M. Easily offended

$\overline{}$ $\overline{}$ $\overline{}$ $\overline{}$ $\overline{}$
62   7   2   30   13

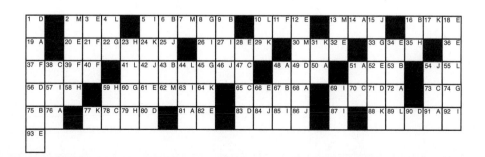

Answers on page 189.

CLASSIC '80S MOVIE: "NASTY HAYING"?

As far as we know, there's no movie by that name. But if you rearrange the letters, you will come up with a 1989 Cameron Crowe film that starred John Cusack and Ione Skye. Unscramble the phrases below to come up with 5 more hits of the '80s:

1. NASTY HAYING

2. REAL CUSHION

3. LIP ARENA!

4. NEBULAR NERD

5. HIGH TENNIS

6. SHORTEST BUGS

Answers on page 189.

TITAN OF TERROR

Cryptograms are messages in substitution code. Break the code to read the message about Alfred Hitchcock. For example, THE SMART CAT might be FVO QWGDF JGF if F is substituted for T, V for H, O for E, and so on.

WUPFHK   IOSXIXLXN   JWB   TLS   LTUR

SIH   AWBSHF   LP   BMBDHTBH,   CMS

SIH   AWHBSFL   LP   JOSSR   FHSLFSB.

SL   W   JLAWT   JIL   XLADUWOTHK

SIWS   SIH   BILJHF   BXHTH   OT

DBRXIL   BL   PFOYISHTHK   IHF

KWMYISHF   SIWS   SIH   YOFU   JLMUK

TL   ULTYHF   BILJHF,   IH   BWOK,

"SIHT   AWKWA,   O   BMYYHBS   RLM

IWZH   IHF   KFR-XUHWTHK."

HERE'S LOOKING AT YOU...

ACROSS

1. Muscles used in situps

4. Bogart's rank as Joe Gunn in "Sahara": abbr.

7. "No problemo!"

12. Hellboy's love

13. Billiard stick

14. Letters opened with a click

15. "Sesame Street" network

16. Sesame product

17. Prepared apples for apple-sauce

18. 1953 Bogart war movie

21. Catwoman portrayer Eartha

22. It might be pale

23. ____ Mountains (Eurasia divider)

25. "____ Stone" (TV series)

26. HBO competitor

29. 1941 Bogart mystery, with "The"

33. NL team, on scoreboards

34. Anti-communist soldier

35. Encourage

36. Was in the forefront

37. Sultry actress Sommer

39. 1951 Bogart adventure, with "The"

44. Believe in

45. "Be ____ Guest" ("Beauty and the Beast" song)

46. Bus alternative

48. Director of "My Dinner with Andre"

49. Wish it weren't so

50. Wellness grp.

51. Noble horse

52. Donkey

53. Nikkei Index currency

DOWN

1. Mont Blanc or Matterhorn

2. Lettuce type

3. He played Carl in "Casablanca"

4. Bogart's leading lady in "Dead Reckoning"

5. ____ trip

6. TV part?

7. Simon and Garfunkel hit

8. Love, Italian-style

9. Ray Liotta movie

10. Almighty, in Alsace

11. GM car until 2004

19. Pinball warning

20. Young cow

23. Actress Thurman

24. ____ Pack (Bogart's friends)

25. Mock cry of horror

26. Like some owls

27. Motorcycle, in slang

28. United

30. Put up

31. Kind of a jerk?

32. "Star Wars" hero

36. Cotton thread

37. Peter Shaffer play

38. Anglers' purchases

39. Money dispensers, for short

40. Traditional hazing site

41. Principle

42. "You've Got Mail" director Ephron

43. "You're not a star until they can spell your ____ in Karachi": Bogart

47. "____ voyage"

Answers on page 190.

STARTING WITH C

Every film title listed is contained within the group of letters. Titles can be found in a straight line horizontally, vertically, or diagonally. They may read either forward or backward.

CABARET

CABIN FEVER

CADDYSHACK

CAKE

CANDYMAN

CAPOTE

CARRIE

CARS

CASABLANCA

CASINO

CAST AWAY

CATS

CHANGELING

CHARIOTS OF FIRE

CHICAGO

CHILD'S PLAY

CHINATOWN

CINDERELLA

CITIZEN KANE

CITY SLICKERS

CLERKS

CLOCKERS

CLOSER

CLOWN

CLUELESS

COCKTAIL

COCOON

COLD MOUNTAIN

COLLATERAL

CONGO

COOL HAND LUKE

CORALINE

CRASH

CREED

CYRUS

```
C O O C O C K T A I L E O C C A R R
A E C L O C K E R S E K R A C A K C
P K N E A C R E H O I U E S C R T A
O C K A R R O E R P R L V I R Y E K
T O C O K I E N L A R D E N E A S E
E L A A G N F T G C A N F O E W R C
I C H C N A E F A O C A N C D A E Y
S C S L S D C Z O L O H I O W T K C
A A Y O C T Y I I S L L B C A S C O
C B D W L L A M H T T O A I T A I R
C A D N W C U C A C I O C L S C L A
Y R A L L E R E D N I C I A A I S L
R E C H A N G E L I N G B R C H Y I
U T C A R S S E L E U L C O A C T N
S N O O C O C Z H S A R C C R H I E
C A B A R N I A T N U O M D L O C U
N W O T A N I H C H I L D S P L A Y
Z C L O S E R A R I S K R E L C L C
```

155　Answers on page 190.

GOODFELLA, GODFATHER, AND FATHER-IN-LAW

Solve the clues below, and then place the letters in their corresponding spots in the grid to reveal a quote from Robert De Niro. The letter in the upper-right corner of each grid square refers to the clue the letter comes from. A black square indicates the end of a word.

A. Corleone homeland

$\overline{24}$ $\overline{68}$ $\overline{35}$ $\overline{50}$ $\overline{9}$ $\overline{88}$

B. Fishy De Niro film?: 2 wds.

$\overline{27}$ $\overline{32}$ $\overline{86}$ $\overline{76}$ $\overline{6}$ $\overline{59}$ $\overline{22}$ $\overline{10}$ $\overline{62}$

C. "Taxi Driver" setting: 3 wds.

$\overline{5}$ $\overline{33}$ $\overline{12}$ $\overline{26}$ $\overline{8}$ $\overline{38}$ $\overline{45}$ $\overline{20}$ $\overline{80}$ $\overline{66}$ $\overline{73}$

D. Fredo and Michael, for example

$\overline{57}$ $\overline{64}$ $\overline{13}$ $\overline{60}$ $\overline{48}$ $\overline{46}$ $\overline{74}$ $\overline{18}$

E. Professional killer

$\overline{7}$ $\overline{44}$ $\overline{83}$ $\overline{52}$ $\overline{17}$ $\overline{78}$

F. 2008 De Niro Film: "_____ Kill"

$\overline{41}$ $\overline{4}$ $\overline{82}$ $\overline{67}$ $\overline{63}$ $\overline{49}$ $\overline{14}$ $\overline{90}$ $\overline{25}$

G. Travis Bickle and Sonny Corleone

$\overline{3}$ $\overline{37}$ $\overline{70}$ $\overline{61}$ $\overline{75}$ $\overline{40}$ $\overline{15}$ $\overline{69}$

H. Finally

$\overline{65}$ $\overline{43}$ $\overline{54}$ $\overline{1}$ $\overline{91}$ $\overline{19}$ $\overline{31}$ $\overline{85}$ $\overline{21}$ $\overline{11}$

I. Police searches

$\overline{30}$ $\overline{34}$ $\overline{79}$ $\overline{16}$ $\overline{58}$ $\overline{51}$ $\overline{36}$ $\overline{56}$

J. Those who participate in sports

$\overline{53}$ $\overline{2}$ $\overline{84}$ $\overline{89}$ $\overline{29}$ $\overline{47}$ $\overline{72}$ $\overline{23}$

K. Excites

$\overline{55}$ $\overline{81}$ $\overline{28}$ $\overline{71}$ $\overline{77}$ $\overline{39}$ $\overline{42}$ $\overline{87}$

Answers on page 190.

DAVID FINCHER MOVIES

ACROSS

1. Ripped, in gym lingo

5. "The ____ Network," 2010 film directed by David Fincher

11. eBay competitor

12. Bet to win and place

13. Sonic the Hedgehog company

14. Corroborate

15. Buckingham Palace monogram

16. Slangy greetings

17. Biblically yours

19. Banned chem. pollutant

22. Embroidery loop

24. Pepys work

26. Fully qualified

27. Macrame basic

28. Like people from Mecca

30. Diva's pride

31. A basketball, but not a football

32. Former French coin

34. Gobsmack

35. Disagreeably damp and chilly

38. Large unit of resistance

41. One may be swinging or sliding

42. Maple leaf, for Canada

43. Zip quantity

44. Like a pitcher's bag

45. "Ditto!"

DOWN

1. Australian wilderness

2. Car-ride company

3. 1999 Brad Pitt film directed by David Fincher

4. Agcy. that approves medicines

5. 1995 Brad Pitt film directed by David Fincher

6. Like Betty Boop

7. Sleepers and diners

8. French "here"

9. Org. that monitors gun sales

10. Put down, as linoleum

16. Perfect-game spoiler

18. Broke soil for planting

19. 2002 Jodie Foster thriller directed by David Fincher

20. Aussie water hazard

21. Eight bits in a computer

22. ____ doble (bullfight music)

23. Building beam

25. Byzantine image

29. Kind of logical statement

30. Family-size vehicle

33. Gin ____ (card game)

34. Arias for one

36. Top-notch

37. Small brown songbird

38. "La ____" (Debussy work)

39. Adjective for "pop punk"

40. "Pygmalion" monogram

41. Genetic fingerprint

Answers on page 191.

NAME IN THE TITLE

Every film title listed is contained within the group of letters. Titles can be found in a straight line horizontally, vertically, or diagonally. They may read either forward or backward.

ALI

AMÉLIE

ANNIE

ANTWONE FISHER

BILLY ELLIOT

CARRIE

COOL HAND LUKE

DAVE

DONNIE DARKO

ERIN BROCKOVICH

FATIMA

FORREST GUMP

FRIDA

G.I. JANE

GANDHI

GOOD WILL HUNTING

HARRIET

I AM SAM

I, TONYA

JACKIE

JERRY MAGUIRE

JOHN WICK

JUDY

LINCOLN

MAD MAX

MARY POPPINS

MULAN

NORMA RAE

OLIVER!

PHILOMENA

RAY

REBECCA

ROSEMARY'S BABY

STEVE JOBS

STILL ALICE

VERA DRAKE

```
F  J  T  F  R  I  D  A  A  S  T  E  V  E  J  O  B  S
W  R  E  B  E  C  C  A  T  M  F  K  Y  D  U  J  F  L
A  J  I  G  R  R  G  A  O  B  E  U  A  O  D  N  A  G
G  M  R  D  I  S  N  R  I  P  R  L  Y  K  E  S  T  J
A  A  R  J  U  N  I  E  L  M  E  D  N  R  K  E  I  A
N  D  A  A  G  I  T  A  L  U  H  N  O  A  A  C  M  N
D  M  H  C  A  P  N  R  E  G  S  A  T  D  R  I  A  E
H  A  W  K  M  P  U  A  Y  T  I  H  I  E  D  L  C  M
I  X  R  I  Y  O  H  M  L  S  F  L  H  I  A  A  L  O
K  A  I  E  R  P  L  R  L  E  E  O  I  N  R  L  I  L
Y  C  L  T  R  Y  L  O  I  R  N  O  F  N  E  L  N  I
O  L  I  J  E  R  I  N  B  R  O  C  K  O  V  I  C  H
A  R  N  W  J  A  W  I  R  O  W  M  A  D  M  T  O  P
N  E  C  M  N  M  D  A  E  F  T  K  C  A  J  S  K  L
N  V  O  U  V  H  O  M  B  T  N  C  A  R  R  I  E  A
I  I  L  L  A  R  O  S  E  M  A  R  Y  S  B  A  B  Y
E  L  N  A  D  L  G  J  C  A  M  E  L  I  E  V  A  D
X  O  E  N  A  J  I  G  N  O  T  I  M  A  S  M  A  I
```

ONLY THE GOOD DIE YOUNG

Change just one letter on each line to go from the top word to the bottom word. Do not change the order of the letters. You must have a common English word or a name at each step.

DEAN

_____ Connery or Penn

_____

_____

_____

_____ violinist Leopold

_____

_____

_____

EDEN

Answers on page 191.

TITLE AND DIRECTOR

Cryptograms are messages in code. Break the code to read 4 films and their directors. For example, THE SMART CAT might be FVO QWGDF JGF if F is substituted for T, V for H, O for E, and so on. The code is the same for each.

1. *KMABL SJ KMABLFTIB:* EPWATR LNBOLOMOV

2. *BLT ILNKNKD:* IBEKPTJ VGSANOV

3. *ONBNQTK VEKT:* MAIMK FTPPTI

4. *AEDNKD SGPP:* XEABNK

DRAW YOUR WEAPON

Unscramble each phrase to find the titles of war films.

1. NATO POL _____

2. GET SPACE HEATER _____

3. CALYPSO WEAPON _____

4. ENTERED HER HUT _____

GENE KELLY

ACROSS

1. Bachelor's place
4. Genetic letters
7. Anjou or Bosc
11. Sash tied in back
12. China neighbor
13. Janis's comic strip mate
14. "____ Girls" (1957 Gene Kelly film)
15. Freeze front?
16. "The Happy ____" (1957 Gene Kelly film)
17. Gene Kelly's partner in "Singin' in the Rain"
20. Wife or husband
22. "____ sad but true"
23. Astringent stuff
24. (As written)
25. Frozen dessert
28. Gene Kelly's costar in "Singin' in the Rain"
32. Likely to catch on quickly
33. ISP with a circle-in-a-triangle logo
34. "My Name Is ____" (TV series)
35. 60 secs.
36. Novelist Charlotte

38. Gene Kelly's partner in "Summer Stock"
42. Cut ____
43. Car that has seen better days
44. "On ____ Little Houseboat" (Gene Kelly/Shirley MacLaine duet)
47. Notion
48. Duplex or studio
49. Ryder Cup team
50. Temporary pause
51. Keatsian "always"
52. Pro ____ (for now)

DOWN

1. Washington type
2. Maggie Simpson's grandpa
3. Reduce in price
4. Emulate Gene Kelly
5. Portrayer of Mr. Big on "Sex and the City"
6. Eastern
7. "An American in ____" (1951 Gene Kelly musical)
8. Arrow shooter of myth
9. Alack's partner
10. Needled

12. Boys

18. "3:10 to ___"

19. "Little Caesar" nickname

20. Tony winner Thompson

21. Fall heavily

24. The Sun

25. Intermittently at home, say

26. Bud of "Harold and Maude"

27. First name in legal fiction

29. "Mare's ___" (gun on "Wanted: Dead or Alive")

30. Talk show giant Phil

31. Broadway light gas

35. "For Me and ___" (Gene Kelly's first movie)

36. Betsy ___, Gene Kelly's first wife

37. Mesmerized

38. Hoosegow

39. Language written in Persian-Arabic letters

40. Fight with Gene Kelly in "The Three Musketeers"

41. French director Clair

45. Customary practice

46. Ewe mate

Answers on page 191.

YOUR 15 MINUTES

Move each of the letters below into the grid to form common words. You will use each letter once. The letters in the numbered cells of the grid correspond to the letters in the phrase at the bottom. Completing the grid will help you complete the phrase and vice versa. When finished, the grid and phrase should be filled with valid words, and you will have used all the letters in the letter set.

Hint: The numbered cells in the grid are arranged alphabetically, so the letter in the cell marked 1 will appear in the alphabet before the letter in the cell marked 2, and so on.

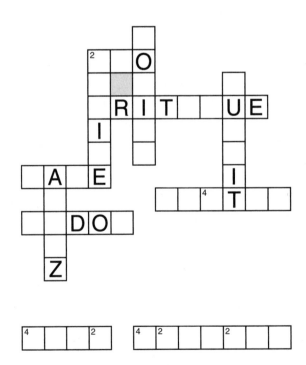

Answers on page 192.

CRYPTOGRAMS

Cryptograms are messages in substitution code. Break the code to read the titles of 8 films directed by Paul Thomas Anderson. For example, THE SMART CAT might be FVO QWGDF JGF if F is substituted for T, V for H, O for E, and so on. These cryptograms share a common cipher.

1. JAHBH UCVV DH DVXXQ

2. DXXKCH SCKAJY

3. JAH TFYJHB

4. TFKSXVCF

5. EAFSJXT JABHFQ

6. EZSIA-QBZSR VXNH

7. CSAHBHSJ NCIH

8. AFBQ HCKAJ

167　　　　　　　　　　　　Answers on page 192.

STARS OF CLASSIC HOLLYWOOD

Every name listed is contained within the group of letters. Names can be found in a straight line horizontally, vertically, or diagonally. They may read either forward or backward.

ASTAIRE (Fred)

BERGMAN (Ingrid)

BETTE DAVIS

BOGART (Humphrey)

BURTON (Richard)

CARY GRANT

CLARK GABLE

CRAWFORD (Joan)

DE HAVILLAND (Olivia)

DIETRICH (Marlene)

DORIS DAY

ERROL FLYNN

EVA MARIE SAINT

GARLAND (Judy)

GRACE KELLY

GRETA GARBO

HENRY FONDA

HEPBURN (Audrey)

HESTON (Charlton)

HUDSON (Rock)

JAMES DEAN

JEAN HARLOW

KIRK DOUGLAS

LAKE (Veronica)

LANA TURNER

LAUREN BACALL

LILLIAN GISH

MARILYN MONROE

MCQUEEN (Steve)

SANDRA DEE

NATALIE WOOD

SIDNEY POITIER

O'HARA (Maureen)

STANWYCK (Barbara)

PAUL NEWMAN

STEWART (James)

PECK (Gregory)

TAYLOR (Elizabeth)

PETER O'TOOLE

TRACY (Spencer)

RITA MORENO

VIVIEN LEIGH

```
B N T P E T E R O T O O L E C E P G N
H E O A U V I V I E N L E I G H H A O
B E R T Y P A U L N E W M A N T U R S
T U P G S L N M R C R A W F O R D L D
R Q R B M E O A A O T R A W E T S A U
A C A T U A H R E R R O L F L Y N N H
C M H B O R N I B D I E T R I C H D C
Y D O E K N N L A U R E N B A C A L L
R E I T I O P Y E N D I S V P A R I A
I H T T R R E N R U T A N A L R A L R
T A N E K A L M T R A G O B I T H L K
A V A D D D O O W E I L A T A N O I G
M I R A O K T N D O R I S D A Y T A A
O L G V U C G R E T A G A R B O N N B
R L Y I G E Y O Y L L E K E C A R G L
E A R S L P J E A N H A R L O W I I E
N N A S A N D R A D E E E R I A T S A
O D C E S T A I A D N O F Y R N E H P
S T A N W Y C K P J A M E S D E A N W
```

Answers on page 192.

ANSWERS

MARVEL-OUS MOVIES (pages 4–5)

T	H	O	R		D	E	F		H	U	L	K
R	E	N	O		E	T	E		O	N	E	A
A	R	K	S		N	O	R		E	A	V	E
C	A	P	T	A	I	N	M	A	R	V	E	L
			R	P	M		E	N	S	O	R	
S	E	T	U	P		E	N	D		W	A	S
M	A	A	M		R	E	T		L	E	G	O
U	R	I		A	Y	E		C	A	D	E	T
	B	L	I	N	K		I	C	Y			
D	O	C	T	O	R	S	T	R	A	N	G	E
O	N	O	S		I	T	S		B	A	R	D
S	E	A	M		S	A	O		E	N	I	D
E	S	T	E		P	R	N		T	A	D	A

ONE TIME (page 7)

```
I  L  L  M  F  I  F  M
L  M  L  M  M  I  M  M
L  L  F  F  I  I  L  M
L  L  M  I  M  I  L  F
F  L  I  I  F  L  L  F
I  F  L  I  L  I  M  L
M  I  M  M  I  F  L  M
M  I  F  L  F  L  I  I
```

THE DARK SIDE (pages 8–9)

A. unique; B. Corpse; C. guava;
D. "Planet of the Apes"; E. bratty;
F. juice; G. virtuosity; H. "Big Fish";
I. mammogram; J. theater; K. meatballs

"There's just something visceral about moving a puppet frame by frame. There's a magical quality about it."

RHYME TIME (page 6)

1. hot tot
2. far star
3. troupe group
4. after laughter
5. space chase
6. past cast or last cast
7. last broadcast
8. Dan fan

KNIVES OUT (pages 10–11)

A	S	A		M	O	M		S	I	R	E	E
T	E	X	T	U	R	E		K	N	O	T	S
A	R	O	U	S	E	S		I	D	E	A	L
D	A	N	I	E	L	C	R	A	I	G		
		L	E	S	A	B	R	E				
P	E	E	L		E	L	I	E		E	O	S
L	E	V	E	E			A	L	L	A	H	
O	L	E		P	A	B	A		I	F	F	Y
		M	I	N	I	C	A	B				
	B	E	S	T	A	C	T	R	E	S	S	
N	E	W	D	O		S	O	L	A	R	I	A
P	L	A	I	D		E	R	A	S	I	N	G
R	O	Y	C	E		D	D	S		E	K	E

ELEVATOR WORDS (page 12)

1. AMAZING Grace
2. Grace Kelly
3. Kelly green
4. green screen
5. screenplay
6. playground
7. ground CONTROL

ADD-A-WORD (page 13)

1. film; 2. shot; 3. sub; 4. crew; 5. character

SAY WHAT? (page 13)

"I started at the top and worked my way down."

LEADING MEN (pages 14–15)

1. Phoenix; 2. Christian Bale;
3. Ryan Gosling; 4. Rami Malek;
5. Brad Pitt; 6. Willem Dafoe;
7. Tom Hanks; 8. DiCaprio;
9. Mahershala Ali; 10. Adam Driver;
11. Matt Damon; 12. Eddie Redmayne

GREAT LINES FROM THE MOVIES (page 16)

1. "Houston, we have a problem."
   —*Apollo 13*
2. "I see dead people."
   —*The Sixth Sense*
3. "Show me the money!"
   —*Jerry Maguire*
4. "Say hello to my little friend."
   —*Scarface*

B_NG J_ _N H_ F_LMS (page 17)

1. "The Host"
2. "Memories of Murder"
3. "Mother"
4. "Okja"
5. "Parasite"
6. "Snowpiercer"

EITHER/OR (page 18)

Eternity/entirety

PASSING A BIRD'S HOME (page 18)

"One Flew Over the Cuckoo's Nest"

CODE-DOKU (page 19)

J	A	W	S
W	S	A	J
A	J	S	W
S	W	J	A

ADAM DRIVER FILMS (pages 20–21)

D	E	P	P		A	L	I		B	T	U	S
C	I	A	O		J	O	N		O	S	S	O
I	N	R	E		A	D	S	L	O	G	A	N
			T	H	E	R	E	P	O	R	T	
	C	E	L	S			A	W	S			
T	H	R	E	A	D	E	D			C	U	E
M	A	R	R	I	A	G	E	S	T	O	R	Y
I	R	E			R	O	S	E	W	I	N	E
		A	R	K			E	O	N	S		
	F	R	A	N	C	E	S	H	A			
I	C	A	N	T	E	L	L		O	B	O	E
W	I	K	I		S	A	L		U	L	N	A
O	G	E	E		S	P	Y		R	E	S	T

BEST ACTRESS WINNERS (pages 24–25)

C	A	M		E	M	M	A		B	R	I	E
O	L	E		Z	E	A	L		L	E	N	A
N	O	W		P	A	I	L		O	R	E	S
J	U	L	I	A	N	N	E	M	O	O	R	E
			A	S	S		G	A	M	U	T	S
B	D	R	M	S		A	R	T		T	I	O
R	I	O	S		O	N	O		S	E	A	U
I	S	T		A	B	T		M	I	D	S	T
T	R	O	M	P	E		T	O	G			
C	A	T	E	B	L	A	N	C	H	E	T	T
H	E	I	R		I	M	O	K		C	O	Y
E	L	L	Y		S	I	T	U		O	R	R
S	I	L	L		K	E	E	P		N	E	E

WALK OF FAME (page 22)

WALK, talk, tale, tame, FAME

LETTER TILES (page 22)

Answers may vary.
1. belt; 2. blob; 3. blur; 4. bolt; 5. buck;
6. bulb; 7. bulk; 8. bust; 9. clot; 10. cork;
11. cost; 12. ebbs; 13. lobs; 14. lock;
15. lose; 16. rest; 17. rock; 18. sect;
19. trek; 20. tube.
(Other possible answers: bloc, blot,
bout, brut, colt, cots, cute, cuts, lest,
lobe, luck, lurk, robe, robs, rubs, rust,
slob, sock, suck, stub, tusk, tubs, tuck.)

2 THUMBS UP (page 23)

1. c) Eyes; 2. c) Madre; 3. d) Eternity;
4. b) Kind; 5. d) Desire; 6. c) Friday;
7. d) Wind; 8. d) Night; 9. a) Queen;
10. b) Man

A TUNEFUL LOVE STORY (pages 26–27)

A. the trolley; B. bamboo; C. Yourself;
D. magnifying; E. Esther; F. whooped;
G. Truett; H. entertaining; I. "You and I";
J. mayhem

"My dear, when you get to be my age,
you'll find out there are more important
things in life than boys."

CRYPTO-QUOTES (page 28)

1. "Toto, I've a feeling we're not in
   Kansas anymore."

2. "I'll get you, my pretty, and your little
   dog, too!"

3. "There's no place like home."

ANAGRAMS (page 29)

1. "Cleopatra"
2. "National Velvet"
3. "A Place In the Sun"
4. "The Taming of the Shrew"
5. "Who's Afraid of Virginia Woolf?"
6. "Suddenly, Last Summer"
7. "Cat On a Hot Tin Roof"
8. "Raintree County"
9. "The Sandpiper"
10. "Giant"

THE BREAKFAST CLUB (pages 30–31)

SUCCESS BECOMES HER (pages 32–33)

The leftover letters spell: "Accidentally left her Oscar on the back of a toilet."

HOLLYWOOD NICE GUY (pages 34–35)

A. vivid; B. You've Got; C. untruth; D. "Toy Story"; E. valve; F. football; G. outwit; H. Wilson; I. Lieutenant; J. Avenue; K. fatherhood; L. afraid

"I love what I do for a living, but you have to survive an awful lot of attention that you don't truly deserve."

ADD-A-WORD (page 36)

1. screen; 2. back; 3. story; 4. type; 5. set; 6. light

BEN-HUR (page 36)

Answers may vary.
BEN, hen, her, HUR

SAY WHAT? (page 37)

"Some of my best leading men have been dogs and horses."

ADDAGRAM (page 37)

The missing letter is C.

"Edward Scissorhands" (1990)
"Schindler's List" (1993)
"Clueless" (1995)
"Titanic" (1997)

DIRECTED BY CLINT EASTWOOD (pages 38–39)

LEADING LADIES (pages 40–41)

1. Johansson; 2. Meryl Streep; 3. Erivo;
4. Emma Stone; 5. Saoirse Ronan;
6. Larson; 7. Lady Gaga; 8. Colman;
9. Julia Roberts; 10. Zellweger;
11. Amy Adams; 12. Nicole Kidman;
13. Theron

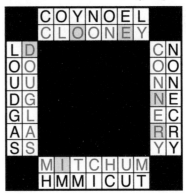

SCRAMBLEGRAM (page 42)

KEYWORD

OEDINR
DENIRO

MORE GREAT LINES FROM THE MOVIES (page 43)

1. "Go ahead, make my day."
   —*Sudden Impact*
2. "Nobody puts Baby in the corner."
   —*Dirty Dancing*
3. "There's no crying in baseball!"
   —*A League of Their Own*
4. "You can't handle the truth!"
   —*A Few Good Men*

ONCE UPON A TIME...IN HOLLYWOOD (pages 44-45)

ELEVATOR WORDS (page 46)

1. INSIDE out
2. out cold
3. Cold Mountain
4. mountaintop
5. Top Gun
6. Gun Crazy
7. Crazy HEART

WORD LADDER (page 47)

CAST, case, care, fare, farm, firm, FILM

MOVIES FROM A TO Z (pages 48-49)

LOVE IS IN THE AIR (page 50)

"I came here tonight because when you realize you want to spend the rest of your life with somebody, you want the rest of your life to start as soon as possible."

CHICK FLICK (page 51)

Crossword solution grid with the following fills:

Row 1: G T F
Row 2: SQUEEZABLE F
Row 3: N S A O F
Row 4: I HURRY W A
Row 5: F J E I
Row 6: F EXCERPT H
Row 7: LOVER S
Row 8: E K
Row 9: DAMSEL
Row 10: R

MOVIE   DRAMA

BEST ACTOR WINNERS (pages 52–53)

R	A	M	I		B	A	H		B	H	A	T
O	P	U	S		U	T	E		I	O	T	A
T	E	N	I	N	O	N	E		G	W	T	W
		G	A	R	Y	O	L	D	M	A	N	
		H	A	S		P	E	A	R			
L	A	O			G	A	R	M	E	N	T	
E	D	D	I	E	R	E	D	M	A	Y	N	E
O	V	E	R	S	E	T			A	W	E	
		T	E	A	M		D	H	S			
	C	O	L	I	N	F	I	R	T	H		
R	A	J	A		A	L	T	H	O	U	G	H
U	P	O	N		N	E	T		R	T	E	S
B	O	Y	D		T	A	Y		K	U	R	T

MAY THE FORCE BE WITH YOU (pages 54–55)

The leftover letters spell: "He's quite clever, you know… for a human being."

LOST IN NEW YORK (pages 56–57)

A. Martin Scorsese; B. mohawk;
C. weenie; D. Harvey; E. Cybill Shepherd;
F. wheresoever; G. De Niro;
H. lawlessness; I. Foster; J. walleye;
K. felonies

"Loneliness has followed me my whole life. Everywhere. In bars, in cars, sidewalks, stores, everywhere. There's no escape."

MAHERSHALA ALI MOVIES
(pages 58–59)

```
A X L E . I S P . A T O Z
B E A M . S P A . C R U E
U R G E . E I N S T E I N
. G R E E N B O O K . . .
. B A A L . R U R . . . .
M A R L B O R O . . P P O
H I D D E N F I G U R E S
O N S . I D L E N E S S .
. M O O . O C T O . . . .
. M O O N L I G H T . . .
S U P P O S E D . A I M S
E S A U . E N O . I F F Y
N E A P . T I L . N Y A D
```

BRAT PACK (page 60)

Answers may vary.
BRAT, beat, bent, rent, rant, rank, rack, PACK

W_S _ND_RS_N F_LMS (page 61)

1. "Bottle Rocket"
2. "The Darjeeling Limited"
3. "Fantastic Mr. Fox"
4. "The Grand Budapest Hotel"
5. "Isle of Dogs"
6. "The Life Aquatic with Steve Zissou"
7. "Moonrise Kingdom"
8. "The Royal Tenenbaums"
9. "Rushmore"

AMERICA'S "PRETTY WOMAN"
(pages 62–63)

A. Denzel; B. Stepmom; C. Kiefer;
D. the Enemy; E. stoves; F. in cahoots;
G. attorney; H. hits it off; I. audition;
J. Fiona; K. harlot

"I don't think I realized that the cost of fame is that it's open season on every moment of your life."

BATMEN (pages 64–65)

```
M I C H A E L K E A T O N
O E L E G O O
P E N P E E R G R O U P
U T H E T L
P L A N A H E A D H E A
U L O C
C H R I S T I A N B A L E
U H Z B
T O T I M A L L E A R S
A Y N I N U
R A P I D F I R E D V D
U E I N T O S
G E O R G E C L O O N E Y
```

HERE'S TO YOU, MRS. ROBINSON
(page 66)

Jack Nicholson, Robert Redford, and Warren Beatty were all considered for the part of Benjamin Braddock that went to Dustin Hoffman.

CODE-DOKU (page 67)

N	I	M	E	C	A
C	E	A	N	M	I
A	N	C	I	E	M
E	M	I	A	N	C
I	C	E	M	A	N
M	A	N	C	I	E

SOME OF THE BEST PICTURES
(pages 68–69)

FILM STAR (page 70)

Answers may vary.
FILM, fill, fell, sell, seal, sear, STAR

HITCHCOCK ANAGRAMS (page 71)

1. "Psycho"
2. "Vertigo"
3. "The Birds"
4. "Dial M for Murder"
5. "Strangers on a Train"
6. "North by Northwest"
7. "Rear Window"

ADDAGRAM (page 71)

The missing letter is N.

"Gangs of New York," "Lincoln," "Phantom Thread," "The Last of the Mohicans"

AT THE MOVIES (pages 72–73)

SAY WHAT? (page 74)

"Westerns are closer to art than anything else in the motion picture business."

UNCONVENTIONAL GENIUS
(page 74)

"My momma always said life was like a box of chocolates. You never know what you're gonna get."

CODE-DOKU (page 75)

C	A	T	R	S	O
S	R	O	T	C	A
T	S	C	A	O	R
A	O	R	C	T	S
O	C	A	S	R	T
R	T	S	O	A	C

MOVIE REMAKES (pages 76–77)

F	A	M	E		P	B	S		P	G	D	N
I	B	I	S	■	L	O	T	■	E	U	R	O
T	E	N	T	S	A	L	E	■	D	A	U	B
■	T	H	E	L	I	O	N	K	I	N	G	■
■	■	S	Y	D	■	C	O	C	A	■	■	■
F	A	R	■	■	H	I	B	A	C	H	I
T	H	E	J	U	N	G	L	E	B	O	O	K
D	I	S	A	V	O	W	■	■	S	E	E	■
■	I	M	E	D	■	M	R	T	■	■	■	■
■	A	S	T	A	R	I	S	B	O	R	N	■
A	L	T	A	■	A	D	D	I	T	I	O	N
D	O	O	R	■	M	O	O	■	A	G	U	E
C	E	R	T	■	A	L	S	■	L	A	N	D

CAN YOU REMAKE THIS REMAKE?
(page 78)

1. "Father of the Bride"
2. Steve Martin

LETTER TILES (page 78)

Answers may vary.
1. lens; 2. line; 3. list; 4. lone; 5. lost;
6. nest; 7. news; 8. newt; 9. nine;
10. owns; 11. sent; 12. silo; 13. snow;
14. test; 15. tilt; 16. toes; 17. town;
18. twin; 19. west; 20. wise.
(Other possible answers: lent, lest, lies, lint, lose, lots, noel, none, nose, owes, sewn, silt, sine, site, slow, sole, sown, stew, stow, tent, ties, tile, tine, tins, tint, tole, tone, tote, tows, twit, twos, welt, went, wilt, wine, wins, woes.)

MAD MAX (page 79)

Answers may vary.
FURY, bury, burn, born, worn, word, lord, load, ROAD

WHO DIRECTED? (pages 80–81)

D	R	A	T			A	H	A	S
A	E	R	I	■	L	I	I	I
S	P	I	E	L	B	E	R	G
H	O	D	G	E	■	I	A	N
■	■	A	T	O	N	C	E
P	R	E	M	I	N	G	E	R
E	O	C	E	N	E	■
S	T	A	■	O	S	C	A	R
T	A	R	A	N	T	I	N	O
E	T	T	U	■	A	N	N	O
R	E	E	D	■	R	E	E	K

AUDREY ANAGRAMS (page 82)

1. "Wait Until Dark"
2. "Roman Holiday"
3. "Love In the Afternoon"
4. "Sabrina"
5. "Breakfast at Tiffany's"
6. "The Nun's Story"
7. "My Fair Lady"
8. "How to Steal a Million"
9. "War and Peace"
10. "Funny Face"

ADDAGRAM (page 83)

The missing letter is H.

"About Schmidt"
"One Flew Over the Cuckoo's Nest"
"The Departed"
"Chinatown"

SAY WHAT? (page 83)

"I used to sit in my dressing room at the studio and wonder just how much longer could I keep making believe."

MATT DAMON MOVIES (pages 84–85)

A	H	O	Y		E	L	M		A	S	H	E
C	O	M	O		R	O	O		B	O	O	M
T	R	I	D	E	N	T	S		O	L	E	O
I	N	T	E	R	S	T	E	L	L	A	R	
			L	A	T		L	A	I	R		
J	O	B			E	L	Y	S	I	U	M	
A	L	A	S		D	O	E		H	U	M	P
M	A	R	T	I	A	N				M	A	G
	E	E	N	Y		L	A	G				
	T	H	E	G	R	E	A	T	W	A	L	L
C	H	A	P		A	P	P	L	E	P	I	E
D	A	N	L		T	E	E		N	I	L	E
S	I	D	E		E	E	L		N	A	T	S

ACTING ICON (pages 86–87)

The leftover letters spell: Nicholson has been nominated for an Oscar in five different decades.

SC_RS_S_ F_LMS (page 88)

1. "The Aviator"
2. "Casino"
3. "The Color of Money"
4. "The Departed"
5. "Gangs of New York"
6. "Goodfellas"
7. "Hugo"
8. "The Irishman"
9. "Raging Bull"
10. "Shutter Island"
11. "Taxi Driver"
12. "The Wolf of Wall Street"

SAOIRSE RONAN MOVIES (pages 90–91)

W	H	I	M		A	S	P		T	A	C	K
H	O	B	O		C	O	E		U	P	D	O
O	P	E	L		H	A	R	D	N	E	S	S
		L	O	S	T	R	I	V	E	R		
	D	I	K	E			O	D	D			
A	C	E	A	W	A	R	D			P	O	I
L	O	V	I	N	G	V	I	N	C	E	N	T
E	N	E			E	S	C	O	R	T	E	D
		H	A	R			R	O	S	A		
	B	Y	Z	A	N	T	I	U	M			
O	L	D	M	O	N	E	Y		T	A	P	A
B	A	R	N		G	A	P		O	R	A	L
I	B	M	S		E	R	E		N	T	W	T

VIVA HOLLYWOOD! (page 89)

STAR
ATTRACTION

LEADING ACTRESSES (page 92)

1	2	3	4	5	6	7	8	9	10	11	12	13
W	I	N	S	L	E	T	B	P	F	X	Y	M
14	15	16	17	18	19	20	21	22	23	24	25	26
K	G	U	A	O	C	R	D	H	V	J	Q	Z

ADDAGRAM (page 93)

The missing letter is R.

"Ford v Ferrari"
"The Irishman"
"Ad Astra"
"Avengers: Endgame"

BIOPIC (page 93)

Answers may vary.
BIO, bin, pin, PIC

LEO IN THE MOVIES (pages 94–95)

```
A H A B   I N A H U R R Y
  A   O   N   Z   B     E
B L O O D D I A M O N D
  V   T   I   L   A     T
T E L L T A L E     T O A D
    E       A         P
I M A G E S     S H I V E R
    I       C       N
A X E L   H A V E A C O W
    I   E   O   I   W   A
    T O T A L E C L I P S E
    U   O   A   E   N   I
O P E N A R M S     K I S S
```

ADD-A-WORD (page 100)

1. star; 2. studio; 3. camera; 4. screen;
5. sound

STILL A HERO (page 100)

Answers may vary.
FORD, fore, sore, sole, SOLO

A PUZZLING PERSPECTIVE
(page 101)

DOCUMENTARY

ACROSTIC ANAGRAM
(pages 96–97)

A. anyway; B. arctic; C. watery; D. tower;
E. chain; F. annoys; G. ozone; H. utility;
I. heaved; J. flank; K. layout; L. vivid

"You can't say that civilization don't
advance . . . for in every war they kill you
a new way."

CINEMATOGRAPHERS
(pages 102–103)

```
E L S W I T E P O P L L I B A D
L I B A T I Q U E K H O N D J I
A T K I K S N I M A K B G P R C
Z T W M L L O T N H O J R E I K
Z O W A L L Y P F I S T E R C P
S N G N E A S N D Q D G O H A O
A I M D Y H L T M I M E G G R P
K P O N O N D A O I O L S T A E
U S R W N D A E R R N U C O R P
L I R I A S H A R S A A B H L D R
G T I A N A N N R N E E A A N I
N R S K M O H O D E Z N N N E E
U E O E R C O A A B K E D K M T
O B R R O Z J S S E I L V I V O
Y L Z D Y K A M E T Y O H N A V
L A C H M A N E R G D N A S N W
```

TOM HANKS MOVIES (pages 98–99)

```
P O S T   B E N   S T L O
N I L E   L I E   C A A N
O L I P H A N T   A I D S
M Y D E A R     S U L L Y
      E W E     U S E S
B E D       G R O U P O N
B R I D G E O F S P I E S
C A S E L A W       N R A
    C H A T   A D V
    C L O U D   B A I L E Y
F E A R   I N C H O A T E
A D I N   R I T   L I O N
D E M S   T A V   A N N S
```

182

CRYPTOGRAMS (page 104)

1. "Roman Holiday"
2. "To Kill a Mockingbird"
3. "The Guns of Navarone"
4. "Spellbound"
5. "The Keys of the Kingdom"
6. "Gentleman's Agreement"
7. "The Yearling"
8. "Twelve O'Clock High"
9. "Cape Fear"
10. "The Omen"

DIRECTOR ANAGRAMS (page 105)

1. Anderson; 2. Bergman; 3. Bigelow;
4. Burton; 5. Cameron; 6. Coppola;
7. Eastwood; 8. Howard; 9. Jackson;
10. Nichols; 11. Scorsese; 12. Soderbergh;
13. Spielberg; 14. Tarantino

GRETA GERWIG (pages 106–107)

F	L	E	W		O	L	A	F		L	A	B
L	O	D	I		P	A	L	L		A	L	E
A	K	I	N		E	U	L	A		D	O	T
W	I	E	N	E	R	D	O	G		Y	E	S
		D	N	A			W	O	M	B		
A	P	H	I	D		G	E	N	U	I	N	E
D	O	U	X		C	A	D		T	R	E	X
D	E	M	I	G	O	D		H	I	D	E	S
		B	E	A	R		K	I	N			
O	W	L		F	R	A	N	C	E	S	H	A
P	O	I		F	O	I	E		E	T	A	L
E	R	N		E	D	D	A		R	A	Z	E
L	E	G		R	E	E	D		S	T	Y	E

ONE TIME (page 108)

I	E	I	M	O	V	E	I
V	O	V	E	M	M	I	O
M	E	M	M	I	E	E	I
I	O	M	M	I	V	V	M
V	I	V	O	M	V	O	M
M	V	I	O	M	I	I	M
M	V	M	E	E	O	I	O
E	O	E	E	I	E	I	I

STAR WARS (page 109)

Answers may vary.
STAR, sear, hear, head, herd, hard, ward,
WARS

PARASITE (pages 110–111)

F	L	Y		B	O	N	G		D	I	S	H
L	O	A		E	L	A	L		E	M	I	R
A	P	P		A	E	R	O		E	P	P	S
B	E	S	T	P	I	C	T	U	R	E		
			W	A	C		T	H	E	R	O	D
D	E	V	I	L		G	I	S		I	O	I
O	V	E	N		I	N	S		G	A	Z	E
F	A	R		E	T	C		A	R	L	E	S
F	L	Y	E	R	S		T	V	A			
		F	E	A	T	U	R	E	F	I	L	M
F	A	I	R		R	V	E	R		P	A	Y
M	U	N	I		U	E	Y	S		A	N	T
S	K	E	E		E	A	S	E		D	A	H

CASABLANCA QUOTES (page 112)

1. "Here's looking at you, kid."
2. "Louis, I think this is the beginning of a beautiful friendship."
3. "Of all the gin joints in all the towns in all the world, she walks into mine."
4. "Play it, Sam. Play 'As Time Goes By.'"
5. "Round up the usual suspects."
6. "We'll always have Paris."

CODE-DOKU (page 113)

O	I	S	N	U	E	F	M	V
N	V	M	F	S	O	U	I	E
F	U	E	M	I	V	S	O	N
S	E	I	V	O	M	N	U	F
V	N	O	U	E	F	M	S	I
M	F	U	I	N	S	V	E	O
U	S	V	E	F	I	O	N	M
I	M	N	O	V	U	E	F	S
E	O	F	S	M	N	I	V	U

THE ORDINARY HERO
(pages 114–115)

BASEBALL ANAGRAMS (page 116)

1. "Moneyball"
2. "The Natural"
3. "Field of Dreams"
4. "The Sandlot"
5. "For the Love ofhe Game"
6. "A League of Their Own"
7. "Major League"
8. "The Rookie"
9. "Eight Men Out"

LETTER TILES (page 117)

Answers may vary.
1. acres; 2. clans; 3. clean; 4. erase; 5. laser; 6. learn; 7. nears; 8. panes; 9. peels; 10. pecan; 11. penal; 12. place; 13. preys; 14. reply; 15. scale; 16. scalp; 17. scene; 18. sleep; 19. spray; 20. yelps. (Other possible answers: canes, cares, crane, crape, creep, crepe, earns, easel, lance, leans, lease, leper, napes, Nepal, panel, plane, plans, plays, pleas, prays, preen, races, relay, repel, scare, scrap, snare, sneer, space, splay, yearn, years.)

ADDAGRAM (page 117)

The missing letter is R.

"American Hustle"
"The Master"
"Nocturnal Animals"
"Arrival"

THE PRINCESS BRIDE (pages 118–119)

1. 1987; 2. William Goldman; 3. 1973;
4. Florin; 5. Westley; 6. Wallace Shawn;
7. Antiope; 8. Guilder; 9. Christopher Guest;
10. Valerie; 11. Moher; 12. Inconceivable;
13. Peter Cook; 14. Disappointment;
15. Domingo

BEST DAY EVER (page 120)

Groundhog Day was not filmed in
Punxsutawney, Pennsylvania, but in
Woodstock, Illinois. Bill Murray was
bitten by the groundhog twice during
shooting.

QUOTE JUMBLE (page 120)

"Everything is funny as long as it
happens to somebody else."

CODE-DOKU (page 121)

U	G	H	I	C	L	F	T	B
C	L	I	T	F	B	G	H	U
B	F	T	G	U	H	I	C	L
L	T	B	H	G	F	U	I	C
H	C	U	L	B	I	T	F	G
G	I	F	C	T	U	B	L	H
I	H	G	B	L	T	C	U	F
T	U	C	F	H	G	L	B	I
F	B	L	U	I	C	H	G	T

BEST PICTURE ANAGRAMS
(pages 122–123)

1. *Lawrence of Arabia*; 2. *Parasite*;
3. *Braveheart*; 4. *Midnight Cowboy*;
5. *Green Book*; 6. *Casablanca*; 7. *Crash*;
8. *Dances with Wolves*; 9. *Schindler's List*;
10. *Forrest Gump*; 11. *Unforgiven*;
12. *Gladiator*; 13. *Chariots of Fire*;
14. *Moonlight*; 15. *Titanic*; 16. *Ordinary
People*; 17. *Spotlight*; 18. *Rain Man*;
19. *Ben-Hur*; 20. *The Shape of Water*;
21. *The King's Speech*; 22. *The Deer
Hunter*; 23. *All About Eve*

ELEVATOR WORDS (page 124)

1. MEN IN Black
2. Black Swan
3. Swan Lake
4. Lake House
5. housebroken
6. Broken Arrow
7. ArrowSMITH

OCEAN'S ELEVEN ANAGRAMS (page 125)

1. George Clooney
2. Brad Pitt
3. Matt Damon
4. Julia Roberts
5. Carl Reiner
6. Elliott Gould
7. Casey Affleck
8. Andy Garcia
9. Bernie Mac
10. Scott Caan

FRANCES MCDORMAND FILMS (pages 126–127)

P	I	T	A		F	A	T	S		D	U	N
A	M	E	N		U	T	A	H		I	V	E
W	H	E	T		E	R	N	O		S	E	A
N	O	M	A	D	L	A	N	D		P	A	T
			R	N	S		E	D	D	A		
A	S	P	C	A		T	R	Y	I	T	O	N
S	E	A	T		P	B	S		A	C	N	E
S	E	R	I	O	U	S		E	P	H	O	D
		A	C	H	T		A	Y	E			
T	A	D		G	U	N	D	E	R	S	O	N
E	L	I		E	P	E	E		P	A	L	L
S	O	S		E	T	A	L		I	D	L	E
T	E	E		Z	O	L	A		N	E	A	R

BLACK PANTHER (pages 128–129)

C_ _N BR_TH_RS (page 130)

1. "The Ballad Of Buster Scruggs"
2. "Barton Fink"
3. "The Big Lebowski"
4. "Blood Simple"
5. "Bridge of Spies"
6. "Burn After Reading"
7. "Fargo"
8. "Gambit"
9. "The Hudsucker Proxy"
10. "Inside Llewyn Davis"
11. "Intolerable Cruelty"
12. "The Ladykillers"
13. "No Country for Old Men"
14. "O Brother, Where Art Thou?"
15. "Raising Arizona"
16. "A Serious Man"
17. "Suburbicon"
18. "True Grit"

LETTER TILES (page 131)

Answers may vary.
1. chair; 2. chart; 3. cheat; 4. chime;
5. chore; 6. cramp; 7. eight; 8. grape;
9. graph; 10. great; 11. grime; 12. heart;
13. merge; 14. morph; 15. north;
16. other; 17. phone; 18. reach; 19. thing;
20. timer. (Other possible answers:
champ, charm, chimp, cream, crime,
crimp, erect, ether, girth, grate, gripe,
grope, heron, hinge, meant, metro,
might, minor, mirth, month, night,
prime, print, prone, prong, retro, right,
ripen, roach, teach, thong, thorn,
there, three, tramp.)

SAY WHAT? (page 131)

"I suppose I have a highly developed capacity for self-delusion, so it's no problem for me to believe I'm somebody else."

MERYL STREEP MOVIES
(pages 132–133)

M	O	C	S		M	A	D		M	P	A	A
S	P	A	T		I	P	A		A	R	M	S
N	A	B	E		S	O	I	T	G	O	E	S
	H	O	P	E	S	P	R	I	N	G	S	
		S	T	Y		Y	S	E	R			
B	A	D		T	O	M			T	A	P	A
T	H	E	L	A	U	N	D	R	O	M	A	T
W	I	F	E		O	R	E		S	T	E	
		A	A	A	A		A	N	T			
	S	U	F	F	R	A	G	E	T	T	E	
W	E	L	L	T	O	D	O		O	N	U	S
E	R	T	E		A	U	F		P	U	R	E
E	A	S	T		R	E	F		S	T	O	W

A DAME WHO WAS ONCE *THE QUEEN* (page 134)

"When you do Shakespeare, they think you must be intelligent because they think you understand what you're saying."

ADDAGRAM (page 134)

The missing letter is T.

"Little Women"
"Marriage Story"
"Knives Out"
"Parasite"

BIG SCREEN LETTERBOX (page 135)

1	2	3	4	5	6	7	8	9	10	11	12	13
M	X	N	S	J	O	L	I	E	V	A	W	F

14	15	16	17	18	19	20	21	22	23	24	25	26
Y	B	T	P	G	C	R	U	Z	H	D	Q	K

NOT A HACK (pages 136–137)

The leftover letters spell: He won an Oscar for his role as Jimmy "Popeye" Doyle in "The French Connection."

FILM CREW (page 139)

Answers may vary.
FILM, fill, fell, felt, feat, flat, flaw, flow, glow, grow, grew, CREW

NOT EXACTLY A "MAN WITH NO NAME" (pages 140–141)

The leftover letters spell: "CLINT EASTWOOD is an anagram of OLD WEST ACTION."

RHYME TIME (page 138)

1. groovy movie
2. injure Ginger
3. views Cruise
4. Toto photo
5. Liz quiz
6. admit Pitt
7. sole role
8. bait Kate

SAY WHAT? (page 142)

"I have my own rules and adhere to them. The rule is simple but inflexible. A James Stewart picture must have two vital ingredients: it will be clean and it will involve the triumph of the underdog over the bully."

BOND ANAGRAMS (page 143)

1. "Diamonds Are Forever"
2. "A View to Kill"
3. "Casino Royale"
4. "Goldfinger"
5. "Die Another Day"
6. "GoldenEye"
7. "Live and Let Die"
8. "Moonraker"
9. "No Time to Die"
10. "Quantum of Solace"
11. "Skyfall"
12. "Thunderball"
13. "Spectre"
14. "The Living Daylights"
15. "Tomorrow Never Dies"

"SHE DID IT THE HARD WAY"
(pages 144–145)

LIGHTS, CAMERA, ACTION!
(pages 146–147)

LOVE OR MONEY (pages 148–149)

A. Danny Boyle; B. swallow; C. TV show;
D. unaware; E. choreographer; F. hinge;
G. trivia; H. eerie; I. heartache; J. haughty;
K. pioneer; L. wallow; M. huffy

"A few hours ago, you were giving chai for the phone wallahs. And now you're richer than they will ever be. What a player!"

CLASSIC '80S MOVIE: "NASTY HAYING"? (page 150)

1. "Say Anything" (1989)
2. "A Chorus Line" (1985)
3. "Airplane!" (1980)
4. "Blade Runner" (1982)
5. "The Shining" (1980)
6. "Ghostbusters" (1984)

TITAN OF TERROR (page 151)

Alfred Hitchcock was not only the master of suspense, but the maestro of witty retorts. To a woman who complained that the shower scene in *Psycho* so frightened her daughter that the girl would no longer shower, he said, "Then Madam, I suggest you have her dry-cleaned."

HERE'S LOOKING AT YOU...
(pages 152–153)

STARTING WITH C (pages 154–155)

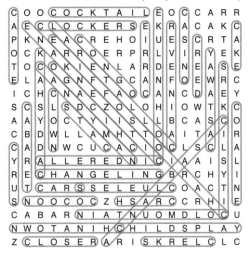

GOODFELLA, GODFATHER, AND FATHER-IN-LAW (pages 156–157)

A. Sicily: B. Shark Tale; C. New York City
D. brothers; E. hitman; F. Righteous
G. hotheads; H. ultimately; I. manhunts
J. athletes; K. enthuses

"I think Hollywood has a class system. The actors are like the inmates, but the truth is they're running the asylum."

DAVID FINCHER MOVIES
(pages 158–159)

B	U	F	F	■	S	O	C	I	A	L
U	B	I	D	■	E	X	A	C	T	A
S	E	G	A	■	V	E	R	I	F	Y
H	R	H	■	H	E	Y	S	■	■	■
■	T	H	I	N	E	■	P	C	B	
P	I	C	O	T	■	D	I	A	R	Y
A	B	L	E	■	■	K	N	O	T	
S	A	U	D	I	■	V	O	I	C	E
O	R	B	■	F	R	A	N	C	■	
■	■	S	T	U	N	■	R	A	W	
M	E	G	O	H	M	■	D	O	O	R
E	M	B	L	E	M	■	N	O	N	E
R	O	S	I	N	Y	■	A	M	E	N

ONLY THE GOOD DIE YOUNG
(page 162)

Answers may vary.
DEAN, Sean, sear, seer, suer, Auer, aver, ever, even, EDEN

TITLE AND DIRECTOR (page 163)

1. *North by Northwest:* Alfred Hitchcock
2. *The Shining:* Stanley Kubrick
3. *Citizen Kane:* Orson Welles
4. *Raging Bull:* Martin Scorsese

DRAW YOUR WEAPON (page 163)

1. Platoon
2. The Great Escape
3. Apocalypse Now
4. The Deer Hunter

NAME IN THE TITLE (pages 160–161)

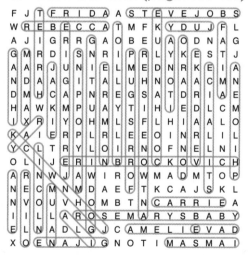

GENE KELLY (pages 164–165)

P	A	D	■	D	N	A	■	P	E	A	R
O	B	I	■	L	A	O	S	■	A	R	L	O
L	E	S	■	A	N	T	I	■	R	O	A	D
■	C	Y	D	C	H	A	R	I	S	S	E	
S	P	O	U	S	E	■	T	I	S			
A	L	U	M	■	S	I	C	■	I	C	E	
D	O	N	A	L	D	O	C	O	N	N	O	R
A	P	T	■	A	O	L	■	E	A	R	L	
■	M	I	N	■	B	R	O	N	T	E		
J	U	D	Y	G	A	R	L	A	N	D		
A	R	U	G	■	H	E	A	P	■	O	U	R
I	D	E	A	■	U	N	I	T	■	U	S	A
L	U	L	L	■	E	E	R	■	T	E	M	

YOUR 15 MINUTES (page 166)

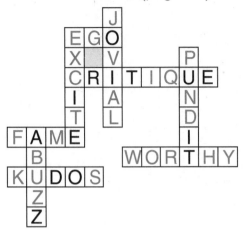

RAVE REVIEWS

STARS OF CLASSIC HOLLYWOOD (pages 168–169)

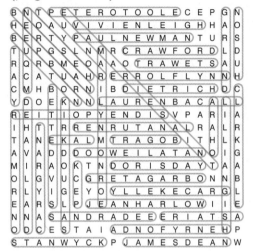

CRYPTOGRAMS (page 167)

1. There Will Be Blood
2. Boogie Nights
3. The Master
4. Magnolia
5. Phantom Thread
6. Punch-Drunk Love
7. Inherent Vice
8. Hard Eight